THE IMMORTAL MESSIAH

THE PHYSIOLOGY OF RESURRECTED BEINGS

WHAT OTHERS ARE SAYING ABOUT THIS BOOK

Dr. Stephens did it again!! He has written another amazing book that bridges religion and science. *The Immortal Messiah* does an outstanding job of blending the two disciplines and shows how they definitely can exist together and aren't opposed to one another. Dr. Stephens has the expertise as a developmental biologist along with an in-depth knowledge of the gospel to help the reader reconcile the relationship between the two.

I was fortunate enough to be one of Dr. Stephens' students years ago. Not only was he the best science instructor I ever had, he also helped me understand the gospel on a deeper level—understanding that God truly is the master biologist, the master chemist, and the master of all truth. This strengthened my comprehension and my faith. *The Immortal Messiah*, along with his other books, is a must read for anyone struggling with attempting to reconcile how science and religion can and do coexist. Thanks, Dr. Stephens!!

—DR. JEFF YBARGUEN, director
Idaho Dental Education Program
Idaho State University

THE IMMORTAL MESSIAH

THE PHYSIOLOGY OF RESURRECTED BEINGS

TRENT DEE STEPHENS, PhD

CFI
An imprint of Cedar Fort, Inc.
Springville, Utah

ISBN 13: 978-1-4621-4345-0

Published by CFI, an imprint of Cedar Fort, Inc.
2373 W. 700 S., Suite 100, Springville, UT 84663
Distributed by Cedar Fort, Inc., www.cedarfort.com

Library of Congress Control Number: 2022941627

Cover design by Courtney Proby

Edited and typeset by Valene Wood

Printed in the United States of America

10 9 8 7 6 5 4 3 2 1

Printed on acid-free paper

This book is dedicated to all those who are seeking a deeper understanding of our Savior Jesus Christ.

OTHER CEDAR FORT BOOKS BY

TRENT DEE STEPHENS

The Infinite Creation: Unifying Science and Latter-day Saint Theology, 2020

The Infinite Fall: A Scientific Approach to the Second Pillar of Eternity, 2021

CONTENTS

PREFACE

By Michael Stark

I first met Dr. Trent Stephens when I stepped onto the campus of Idaho State University as a student for the second time in 1994, not as a newly minted freshman like my first ISU experience in 1986, but as a master's student in Biology, now determined to learn the sciences of life! He began training me during that two-year experience, and the training has never stopped, continuing even now, learning new insights from my first few glances and this book, *The Immortal Messiah*. Importantly, in the pre-publication chapters that I read, the focus is very scripturally centered, and I believe this is "spot on" the right approach. Knowing Trent and his knowledge and belief in the restoration of the gospel, it's not surprising that he always defers to ancient and modern revelation as his guideposts.

As a developmental biologist who has studied the cellular and molecular processes of embryogenesis, and as an anatomist, Trent has gained knowledge of the entire life cycle of the human body from conception to death. More importantly, he is always focused on understanding the gospel of Jesus Christ through study, faith, and prayer. This focus, along with his scientific training and career, his interest in exploring the unknown, and his passion for teaching, together contribute to a powerful way of distilling new ideas regarding difficult to understand gospel topics. Trent's early work with co-author Jeff Meldrum produced the book *Evolution and Mormonism: A Quest for Understanding*, which was a timely exploration of what science has taught us about the creation of life. More recent works (*The Infinite*

Creation and *The Infinite Fall*) have explored the creation and the fall in a more focused way, and I believe prepared him with a deeper knowledge and understanding to now be able to write *The Immortal Messiah*. This look at immortality aligns strongly with the desire that many of us have to understand the Atonement of Jesus Christ as it applies to the resurrection, a difficult topic that many would approach with trepidation. Not Trent Stephens! In this book, he confidently explores scriptural examples of life, death, and the resurrection, aligning them with his scientific knowledge about how our mortal bodies function. Though his confidence in approaching this subject may seem a proud attempt at claiming knowledge and truth, Trent is actually one of the most teachable human beings I know. Specifically, he is always anxious to be corrected, and excited when his past conclusions have been proven wrong! I remember a conversation where Trent and I were debating a difficult topic, and he said, "This is what I've concluded from all the data. In the next life I may be shown that I was completely wrong, and that's fabulous!" He truly loves to learn and teach! Perhaps a clearer way to say it is: "Trent has a passion for always seeking the truth, especially when discovered truth corrects prior dogma." I hope you will read with as much excitement for learning new ideas as he has living and learning each day!

—Michael Stark, PhD
Professor, department chair
Cell Biology and Physiology
Brigham Young University

INTRODUCTION

After the Last Supper and Judas had departed to betray the Savior, Jesus prayed to the Father on behalf of the remaining eleven apostles. During that prayer He said, "And this is life eternal, that they might know thee the only true God, and Jesus Christ, whom thou hast sent."[1] In the conversation leading up to that prayer, speaking to Thomas, the Savior said,

> If ye had known me, ye should have known my Father also: and from henceforth ye know him, and have seen him.
>
> Philip saith unto him, Lord, shew us the Father, and it sufficeth us.
>
> Jesus saith unto him, Have I been so long time with you, and yet hast thou not known me, Philip? he that hath seen me hath seen the Father; and how sayest thou then, Shew us the Father?[2]

Unfortunately, that scripture, perhaps more than any other, has caused an enormous amount of misunderstanding throughout the history of Christianity. The confusion caused by taking this scripture literally rather than metaphorically has led to the abominable creed of the Trinity.[3]

When Joseph Smith entered the grove of trees near his family home in the early spring of 1820 to ask the questions, "Who of all these parties are right; or, are they all wrong together? If any one of them be right, which is it, and how shall I know it?"[4] He was apparently not questioning the common Christian belief in the Trinity; but what he saw that morning would change forever our understanding of the Godhead:

> I saw a pillar of light exactly over my head, above the brightness of the sun, which descended gradually until it fell upon me. . . . When the light rested upon me I saw two Personages, whose brightness and glory defy all description, standing above me in the air. One of them spake unto me, calling me by name and said, pointing to the other—*This is My Beloved Son. Hear Him!*[5]

In several other accounts of this vision, Joseph said that the two looked identical to each other.[6] There is little wonder, then that Jesus would say to His apostles in Jerusalem, "he that hath seen me hath seen the Father."

In our ordinary lives, it is common for a son to be "the spitting image" of his father. When I attend my Stephens and Stones family reunions, many of my cousins delight in calling me "Ray"—my father's name—because I look very much like him when he was nearly my age. I politely reply, "Thank you." I recently attended my fiftieth high school reunion and greeted several classmates I had not seen since graduation day. More than one of them commented, "You look more like your father than you do yourself." I could easily say to a stranger I meet, "If you want to know what my father looked like, just look at me. If you've seen me, you've seen my father."

The Prophet Joseph Smith gave the following instruction to the Saints gathered at Ramus, Illinois, 2 April 1843: "The Father has a body of flesh and bones as tangible as man's; the Son also."[7]

Therefore, we can look to the characteristics of Jesus's resurrected, immortal body in order to understand God's eternal, immortal body. Furthermore, we will all be partakers of the resurrection. As Paul wrote to the Corinthians,

> If in this life only we have hope in Christ, we are of all men most miserable. But now is Christ risen from the dead, and become the firstfruits of them that slept. For since by man came death, by man came also the resurrection of the dead. For as in Adam all die, even so in Christ shall all be made alive.[8]

Therefore, what we learn of God and Christ's physical immortal nature, we also learn of our own future resurrected physical natures.

"In the presence of six elders, at Fayette, New York, September 1830," the following message was revealed to us through the Prophet Joseph Smith, "And thus did I, the Lord God, appoint unto man the days of his probation—that by his natural death he might be raised in immortality unto eternal life, even as many as would believe."[9] Then, on 27 December 1832, in Kirtland, Ohio, the Prophet Joseph Smith received this revelation, "This Comforter is the promise which I give unto you of eternal life, even the glory of the celestial kingdom."[10] Immortality is a free gift given to every human being ever born, whereas eternal life in the celestial kingdom, in God's presence, is obtained by coming to know Jesus Christ through faith, repentance, and obtaining the sacred ordinances pertaining to eternal life.[11]

President Harold B. Lee provided the following definition of eternal life in the October 1966 general conference:

> And this thing called eternal life is to have so lived that one would, by his living, have been counted worthy of eternal life in the presence of God the Father and the Son. . . . From the scriptures, from the writings of inspired Church leaders, and from secular commentaries, eternal life may be defined as life in the presence of those eternal Beings, God the Father and His Son Jesus Christ. To shorten that definition, we might then say that eternal life is God's life. . . . To eventually attain to this celestial excellence should be the never-ending quest of all mortal beings.[12]

In general conference on Easter Sunday, 1 April 2018, President Russell M Nelson testified to the reality of the Savior's—and our—resurrection:

> He was crucified on Calvary's cross and rose the third day as the first resurrected being of our Heavenly Father's children. I love Him and testify that He lives! It is He who leads and guides His Church. . . . Without His Resurrection, death would be the end. Our Savior's Atonement made eternal life a possibility and immortality a reality for all. . . . On

> this Easter Sunday, we commemorate His atoning sacrifice, His literal Resurrection, and His divinity.[13]

In a talk given on 6 May 2001 as part of the 75th anniversary celebration of the Institute of Religion program at a Church Educational System fireside near the University of Idaho campus in Moscow, Idaho, Elder Henry B. Eyring stated,

> The purpose of God's creations and of His giving us life is to allow us to have the learning experience necessary to come back to live with Him in eternal life. . . . The real life we're preparing for is eternal life. Secular knowledge has for us eternal significance. Our conviction is that God, our Heavenly Father, wants us to live the life that He does. . . . All we can learn that is true while we are in this life will rise with us in the Resurrection. And all that we can learn will enhance our capacity to serve.[14]

The purpose of this book is to bring forward the spiritual and secular knowledge I have gained from teaching and researching human anatomy, physiology, and developmental biology for more than forty years to enhance and enlighten our understanding of our Lord and Savior Jesus Christ's mortal and immortal physical body that we might more fully know, "the only true God, and Jesus Christ, whom thou hast sent."[15] In addition to my teaching and research, I have coauthored some fifteen textbooks of Human Anatomy and Physiology. I have been an active and fully committed member of The Church of Jesus Christ of Latter-day Saints my entire life. I am a high priest who has served twice as a bishop and, along with my darling wife, as a temple worker in the Idaho Falls Temple. We now serve in the Pocatello, Idaho Temple.

What do we know about Jesus Christ's immortal physical body? One event that occurred on the first evening after Christ's resurrection assures us that we actually know a lot about the Savior's resurrected body. After the apostles and other disciples were invited to handle the Savior's resurrected body and behold the wounds in his hands and feet, He "did eat before them."[16] Christ ate before His disciples because God commanded Him to do so.[17] Therefore, we must assume that God wanted Christ's disciples *and us* to know that Christ's resurrected body was capable of eating. His disciples in approximately AD 33 would not have comprehended the significance of Jesus eating after His resurrection, because they didn't comprehend the process of eating in themselves. However, today, we know a huge amount about the physiology of eating, and its implications for what we can know about the anatomy and physiology of a resurrected being are enormous. Those implications are the substance of *The Immortal Messiah.*

Two of my favorite scriptures from the Doctrine and Covenants state, "The glory of God is intelligence, or, in other words, light and truth,"[18] and "Whatever principle of intelligence we attain unto in this life, it will rise with us in the resurrection. And if a person gains more knowledge and intelligence in this life through his diligence and obedience than another, he will have so much the advantage in the world to come."[19] It is in the spirit of these scriptures that I offer this book. It is my prayer that the words written in this book will enhance not only the reader's secular understanding of God's, and Christ's, and our own eternal immortal nature; but also enhance his or her spiritual understanding of the scriptures pertaining to that nature.

---

1. John 17:3.
2. John 14:7–9.
3. See Joseph Smith—History 1:19.
4. Joseph Smith History 1:10.
5. Joseph Smith History 1:16–17.
6. "Accounts of Joseph Smith's First Vision," *The Joseph Smith Papers,* Last updated 6 Apr. 2021, josephsmithpapers.org/site/accounts-of-the-first-vision.
7. Doctrine and Covenants 130:22.
8. 1 Corinthians 15:19–22.
9. Doctrine and Covenants 29:43.
10. Doctrine and Covenants 88: 4.
11. c.f. Doctrine and Covenants 76.
12. Lee, President Herald B., "Eternal Life," *Instructor,* Oct. 1966, 378.
13. Nelson, Russell M., "Revelation for the Church, Revelation for Our Lives," Apr. 2018 general conference.
14. Eyring, Henry B., "Education for Real Life," *Ensign,* Oct. 2002.
15. John 17:3.
16. Luke 24:39–43.
17. See John 5:19; 8:28.
18. Doctrine and Covenants 93:36.
19. Doctrine and Covenants 130:18–19.

CHAPTER 1

THE WORD

According to the King James translation of John 1:1–3, we are told that, "In the beginning was the Word, and the Word was with God, and the Word was God. The same was in the beginning with God. All things were made by him; and without him was not any thing made that was made."[1] These three verses are wonderful, classic examples of the beautiful Elizabethan poetry with which the King James Bible is so richly adorned. I love poetry, I love the poetry of the King James Bible, and I love the poetry of those three verses. Unfortunately, however, because of the deep use of metaphor in poetry, the true meaning is often masked by the meter.

The Prophet Joseph Smith has provided us with a far less poetic, but much more accurate translation of those verses, "In the beginning was the *gospel preached through the Son. And the gospel was the word,* and the *word* was with *the Son, and the Son was with God,* and the *Son* was *of* God. The same was in the beginning with God. All things were made by him; and without him was not anything made which was made."[2]

The term in the original Greek, from which the King James Version was translated as "word," is λόγος (*logos*). According to James Strong's Bible Concordance, the term *logos* is "the expression of a thought." It was often used to describe a "person sharing a message." The word logos appears 330 times in the New Testament and has been translated as: a word (as embodying an idea), a statement, a speech, a divine utterance, communication, or an analogy.[3] Thus, the term "gospel," as "preached through the Son," in Joseph Smith's translation conveys the much deeper, broader, and accurate meaning of the word logos; whereas the term "word" employed in the King James Bible allows for the more succinct, although more metaphorical, metered application of the poetry.

According to Hugh Nibley, Aristotle employed the term *logos*, from which is derived the suffix "-ology," to mean "word," "inquiry," or "rationality." Nibley stated,

> The quest for a knowledge of the nature of the First Things [more commonly now called the First or Final Cause], beginning with and hence grounded in the inquiry into nature, is commonly known as ontology (*on*, being, and *logos*, inquiry). . . . Logos (word, inquiry, and hence rationality), or how one can come to know the nature of things, was known as the "second part of philosophy . . . [and] were included within the category of theoretical inquiries by Aristotle."[4]

In other words, the term *logos*, as employed today, means the "study of" or the "science of." Thus we derive the term theology to define our rational inquiry into the nature of God, and the term biology to define our rational inquiry into the nature of living things—"bio-" meaning two, referring to both plants and animals. The term "physiology" refers to the study of how our bodies function.

Today, we may combine the logos of theology, biology, and physiology into one rational understanding of ontology. President Dieter F. Uchtdorf stated in a February 2018 *Ensign* article,

> I want to emphasize that the truth embraced by The Church of Jesus Christ of Latter-day Saints . . . extends beyond time and space and encompasses all truth. . . . The gospel of Jesus Christ encompasses not only the truth of what was and what is but also the truth of what can and will be. It is the most practical of all truths. It teaches the way of the disciple—a path that can take ordinary, flawed mortals and transform them into glorious, immortal,

> and limitless beings whose divine potential is beyond our meager capacity to imagine. . . . The pursuit, discovery, and application of truth are what we are on this earth to discover. . . . Isn't it a remarkable feeling to belong to a Church that embraces truth—no matter the source—and teaches that there is much more to come, that God "will yet reveal many great and important things pertaining to the Kingdom of God"? [Articles of Faith 1:9].[5]

Brigham Young said,

> [The gospel] embraces every fact there is in the heavens and in the heaven of heavens—every fact there is upon the surface of the earth, in the bowels of the earth, and in the starry heavens; in fine, it embraces all truth there is in all the eternities of the Gods. . . . "Mormonism" embraces all truth that is revealed and that is unrevealed, whether religious, political, scientific, or philosophical.[6]

Therefore, according to Brigham Young, the theology of The Church of Jesus Christ of Latter-day Saints incorporates all "-ologies," whether theology, politicology, logology, or hodology. Indeed, we are admonished in the Doctrine and Covenants to

> Teach ye diligently and my grace shall attend you, that you may be instructed more perfectly in theory, in principle, in doctrine, in the law of the gospel, in all things that pertain unto the kingdom of God, that are expedient for you to understand;
>
> Of things both in heaven [uranology] and in the earth [topology], and under the earth [geology]; things which have been [paleontology, anthropology], things which are [currentology], things which must shortly come to pass [futurology]; things which are at home [oikology], things which are abroad [xenology]; the wars [polemology] and the perplexities of the nations [politicology], and the judgments which are on the land [loimology]; and a knowledge also of countries and of kingdoms [cartology]—

> That ye may be prepared in all things when I shall send you again to magnify the calling whereunto I have called you, and the mission with which I have commissioned you.[7]

Thus, for members of The Church of Jesus Christ of Latter-day Saints, for whom the "the glory of God is intelligence"[8] and who believe that "whatever principle of intelligence we attain unto in this life, it will rise with us in the resurrection,"[9] through theology and all the other "-ologies," the logos, we may learn deep, and previously hidden, knowledge of the "Word." The more we learn of our Savior Jesus Christ at this time, the more prepared we will be to "see him as he is" "when he shall appear."[10]

In the April 1844 general conference of the Church, the Prophet Joseph Smith taught the following:

> The mind or the intelligence which man possesses is co-equal with God himself . . . The intelligence of spirits had no beginning, neither will it have an end . . . There never was a time when there were not spirits; for they are co-equal [co-eternal] with our Father in heaven . . . The first principles of man are self-existent with God . . . Intelligence is eternal and exists upon a self-existent principle. It is a spirit from age to age, and there is no creation about it.[11]

Members of The Church of Jesus Christ of Latter-day Saints understand that the term "intelligence"[12] has at least three interconnected meanings:

1. Intelligence is the light of truth, which gives life and light to all things in the universe.[13] It was not created because it has always existed.[14]
2. The spirit children of God are sometimes referred to as intelligences. They are also referred to as souls and spirits.[15]
3. Intelligence is the uncreated, eternal element from which the spirit children of God were created.[16]

1. John 1:1–3.
2. JST John 1:1–3.
3. Strong, James, "logos," *Bible Concordance*, found at "3056. logos," *Bible Hub*, biblehub.com/greek/3056/logos.htm.
4. Midgley, Louis, Hugh W. Nibley, *The Ancient State: The Rulers and the Ruled, Review of Books on the Book of Mormon 1989–2011*, 11 (1), 1999.
5. Uchtdorf, Dieter F., "The Gospel Encompasses All Truth," *Ensign*, Feb. 2018.
6. Young, Brigham, *Journal of Discourses*, vol. 9, 149.
7. Doctrine and Covenants 88:78–80.
8. Doctrine and Covenants 93:36.
9. Doctrine and Covenants 130:18.
10. 1 John 3:2.
11. *Teachings of the Prophet Joseph Smith*, comp. by Joseph Fielding Smith (Salt Lake City, Utah: Deseret Book, 1938), 353–54.
12. "Intelligence, Intelligences," *Guide to the Scriptures*, churchofjesuschrist.org/study/scriptures/gs, retrieved 17 Dec. 2019.
13. Doctrine and Covenants 88:6–13.
14. Doctrine and Covenants 93:29.
15. Abraham 3:21–23.
16. Abraham 3:22; Doctrine and Covenants 76:24.

CHAPTER 2

PREMORTAL SPIRITS

The first two sentences in Lesson 1 of *Preach My Gospel, A Guide to Missionary Service*, state, "God is our Heavenly Father. We are His children." The 2004 First Presidency Message in the front of that book states, "*Preach My Gospel* is intended to help you be a better-prepared, more spiritually mature missionary and a more persuasive teacher."[1] These first two sentences are intended as the introduction to The Church of Jesus Christ of Latter-day Saints for anyone who wants to know about Jesus Christ's Church in these latter days.

These two sentences identify those of us who are members of the Church as unique among Christians right from the beginning. Mainstream trinitarian Christians, i.e. anyone who accepts as doctrine the decision of the First Council of Nicaea in AD 325 concerning the Trinity, believe in "the Father almighty, maker of heaven and earth, of all things visible and invisible," and "in one Lord Jesus Christ, the Only Begotten Son of God, born of the Father before all ages . . . consubstantial with the Father."[2] This sense of "Father" as our maker places us in the same relationship with God the Father as was Pinocchio with the woodcarver Geppetto. Furthermore, mainstream Christian belief holds that only Jesus Christ was "born of the Father before all ages [i.e. before time began, and is] . . . consubstantial with the Father" so that only Jesus Christ is a literal child of God and in some unexplained, mysterious way, Jesus Christ was his own father.[3]

According to mainstream Christian belief, none of us are actually spirit children of God.

The first lesson in *Preach My Gospel* states, "Heavenly Father has provided us, His children, with a way to be successful in this life and to return to live in His presence."[4] The implication that we, as God's children, can "return to live in His presence" is that we were previously in His presence before we were born to earthly parents, and thus can return to His heavenly presence. Indeed, that is our belief. That belief is completely consistent with the statement in Ecclesiastes 12:7, "Then shall the dust return to the earth as it was: and the spirit shall return unto God who gave it."

There are actually six Old Testament scriptures listed in the Topical Guide under the heading "Man, Antemortal Existence of:"[5]

Numbers 16:22—"And they fell upon their faces, and said, O God, the God of the spirits of all flesh, shall one man sin, and wilt thou be wroth with all the congregation?"

This scripture, however, does not state that our spirits are God's offspring nor that they had a premortal existence.

Numbers 27:16—"Let the Lord, the God of the spirits of all flesh, set a man over the congregation." The same may be said of this scripture.

Job 38:7—"When the morning stars sang together, and all the sons of God shouted for joy?" This is one of the most commonly quoted Old Testament scriptures cited as evidence of a pre-existence. However, why does the sentence end in a question mark rather than a period, as would be expected if this were a statement? The answer is, this is not a statement, but rather a challenge from God to Job asking him why he dares to question God's doings. We may read the scripture in context:

> Then the Lord answered Job out of the whirlwind, and said, Who is this that darkeneth counsel by words without knowledge? Gird up now thy loins like a man; for I will demand of thee, and answer thou me. Where wast thou when I laid the foundations of the earth? declare, if thou hast understanding. Who hath laid the measure thereof, if thou knowest? or who hath stretched the line upon it?

> Whereupon are the foundations thereof fastened? or who laid the corner stone thereof; When the morning stars sang together, and all the sons of God shouted for joy?[6]

The challenge of these verses appears to claim that Job wasn't there when the Lord "laid the foundations of the earth," or at least didn't remember that he was there.

Ecclesiastes 12:7 [already cited]—"Then shall the dust return to the earth as it was: and the spirit shall return unto God who gave it." This scripture is clearly referring to a person's death and, again should be read in context:

> Remember now thy Creator in the days of thy youth, while the evil days come not . . . [before] desire shall fail: because man goeth to his long home, and the mourners go about the streets . . . Then shall the dust return to the earth as it was: and the spirit shall return unto God who gave it.[7]

This scripture is quite informative in that it not only states that "the spirit shall return unto God who gave it," but that, through death, "man goeth to his long home." This latter statement clearly suggests that our true home is with God, from whence our spirit came and to where it will return.

Jeremiah 1:4–5—"Then the word of the Lord came unto me, saying, Before I formed thee in the belly I knew thee; and before thou camest forth out of the womb I sanctified thee, and I ordained thee a prophet unto the nations." This is another scripture often cited to support the concept of a premortal existence. Some theologians have dismissed it as such suggesting that it only refers to God's foreknowledge of Jeremiah's mission as a prophet. However, although God's foreknowledge alone could explain how God knew Jeremiah, it does not explain how God sanctified him and ordained him "a prophet unto the nations." Such a statement suggests a premortal covenant between God and Jeremiah—even by the laying on of hands.

Zechariah 12:1—"The burden of the word of the Lord for Israel, saith the Lord, which stretcheth forth the heavens, and layeth the foundation of the earth, and formeth the spirit of man within him."

This scripture leaves no doubt but that God "formeth the spirit of man," but it does not state *when* that formation occurred.

Therefore, of the six scriptures cited, Ecclesiastes 12:1–7 and Jeremiah 1:4–5 appear to be the most convincing that our spirits were "given" by God, were at "home" with him whence thy shall return, and that some of us, at least Jeremiah, were sanctified and ordained by Him to perform certain missions here on earth. Considering the word "gave" in Ecclesiastes, the Hebrew word הָנָתְנ (ne·ta·nah) may mean to give (thus "gave" in Ecclesiastes 12:7), put, set, or provide.[8] Therefore, we may say that God "provided" spirits for our bodies, but there is no implication in this verse of any relationship, such as God being the father of our spirits.

However, the Psalmist wrote that "God [who] standeth in the congregation of the mighty; [and who] . . . judgeth among the gods . . . [stated] I have said, Ye are gods; and all of you are children of the most High."[9] This Psalm implies that at least some of the Jews at the time when this Psalm was written had an understanding of our familial relationship to God—not simply as puppets fashioned by a Supreme Being but actual gods and children of God.

In their book, *The Christ Who Heals*, Fiona and Terryl Givens have stated that:

> Versions of this understanding of an everlasting covenant made in heavenly courts before earth's creation survived in some Jewish understanding and the Jewish culture out of which Christianity arose. It was one of the key tenets of a primordial gospel that those chosen people preserved and taught. "The idea of a covenant between a deity and a people is unknown from other religions and cultures," notes the *Encyclopedia Judaica*. In some Jewish traditions, the righteous souls were "called together by God before he created the universe." Traces of this original understanding persisted in Jewish thought for some time.[10]

In addition, Paul, in writing to the Hebrews, stated, "Furthermore we have had fathers of our flesh which corrected us, and we gave them reverence: shall we not much rather be in subjection unto the Father of spirits, and live?"[11] In making such a statement, Paul was apparently referring to a commonly held belief among the Jews that God is the Father of our spirits. Most Biblical commentators dismiss an actual parent-child relationship being implied here, suggesting that God is our "Father" only by reason of His being our creator (i.e. the Pinocchio—Geppetto relationship). However, it cannot be denied that Paul here is making a direct comparison between the fathers of our physical bodies and the Father of our spirits.

Paul told the Athenians on Mar's Hill, "For in him [God] we live, and move, and have our being; as certain also of your own poets have said, For we are also his offspring. Forasmuch then as we are the offspring of God, we ought not to think that the Godhead is like unto gold, or silver, or stone, graven by art and man's device."[12]

Charles Ellicott commented on the phrase "as certain also of your own poets have said" in his *A New Testament Commentary for English Readers*, published in 1878:[13]

> The quotation has a special interest as being taken from a poet who was a countryman of St. Paul's. Aratus, probably of Tarsus (circ. B.C. 272), had written a didactic poem under the title of Phenomena, comprising the main facts of astronomical and meteorological science as then known. It opens with an invocation to Zeus, which contains the words that St. Paul quotes. Like words are found in a hymn to Zeus by Cleanthes (B.C. 300). Both passages are worth quoting:
>
> "[. . .] And all in all things need we help of Zeus,
> For we too are his offspring."
>
> —Aratus, Phænom. 1–5.
>
> "[. . .] Almighty and for ever, thee, O Zeus, [. . .]
> For we thine offspring are, and we alone
> Of all that live and move upon this earth,
> Receive the gift of imitative speech."
>
> —Cleanthes, Hymn to Zeus.

> The fact of the quotation would at once quicken the attention of the hearers. They would feel that they had not to deal with an illiterate Jew, like the traders and exorcists who were so common in Greek cities, but with a man of culture like their own, acquainted with the thoughts of some at least of their great poets.[14]

Concerning the phrase, "We are also his offspring," Ellicott stated,

> We too often think of the quotation only as happily introduced at the time; but the fact that it was quoted shows that it had impressed itself, it may be, long years before, on St. Paul's memory. As a student at Tarsus it had, we may well believe, helped to teach him the meaning of the words of his own Scriptures: "I have nourished and brought up children" (Isaiah 1:2). The method of St. Paul's teaching is one from which modern preachers might well learn a lesson. He does not begin by telling men that they have thought too highly of themselves, that they are vile worms, creatures of the dust, children of the devil. The fault which he finds in them is that they have taken too low an estimate of their position. They too had forgotten that they were God's offspring, and had counted themselves, even as the unbelieving Jews had done (Acts 13:46) "unworthy of eternal life."[15]

Paul obviously agreed with the poem, however, applying it to Jehovah, not Zeus, as had the mistaken Athenian poets, for he followed the quote by stating, "Forasmuch then as we are the offspring of God, we ought not to think that the Godhead is like unto gold, or silver, or stone, graven by art and man's device."[16] Furthermore, Paul declared, "Whom therefore ye ignorantly worship, him declare I unto you."[17]

Fiona and Terryl Givens have pointed out that "fragmented memories of that heavenly prelude to our earthly life appear in the world's most ancient religions and belief systems. Mesopotamian creation narratives, Greek myths and philosophy, and early Jewish texts all make reference to a life in the spirit before embodiment."[18]

In addition, some of the most prominent early Christian thinkers retained at least fragmentary concepts of a premortal world of spirits. The foremost of those was Origen of Alexandria, who wrote approximately 2,000 treatises during the first half of the third century, was one of the most influential people in early Christian theology, and was described as "the greatest genius the early church ever produced."[19]

John McGuckin, who edited *The Westminster Handbook to Origen* in 2004, said that Origen was "a theologian whom Jerome once described as clearly the most important Christian thinker since the generation of the apostles." McGuckin said that not only was Origen "the Christian church's first and greatest biblical scholar," but he was also "the Christian church's first great mystic, describing the soul's fearful search for its lost Lord." In many parts of the early Christian world, Origen was regarded as the ultimate authority on theological matters. [20]

According to McGuckin,

> [Origen had] a grand passion to tell the epic tale of God's first creation (long before the earth was made), when all rational life was gathered in harmony around the Divine logos (the source of all reasonable intelligence) to comprise the chorus of superangelic spirits . . .each and every soul on earth was for him, once a great and preexistent spirit who had (only recently in God's time) fallen into cosmic sorrow because of their lapse from contemplation.[21]
>
> [Origen's] influence over monastic asceticism was so powerful three centuries after his death that it brought down on his head a posthumous condemnation, for all the agitation it had caused . . .
>
> But despite the devastation of the textual tradition of his works, Origen's manuscripts were still copied and circulated (like samizdat literature), and he always kept a body of Christian admirers who were themselves powerful voices in the formation of Christian theology in their own generations.[22]

In his book, *Church History, A Complete History of the Catholic Church to the Present Day*, John Laux stated that Origen was "known far and wide as the intellectual leader of the Christians." However, "Origen was condemned by the Fifth General Council (553), because it was found that his writings contained a number of heretical doctrines, such as the pre-existence of souls and the final salvation of all men."[23]

However, Origen's notion that "each and every soul on earth was . . .once a great and preexistent spirit who had . . .fallen into cosmic sorrow"[24] is much different in its final conclusion from the belief held by members of The Church of Jesus Christ of Latter-day Saints that each and every soul on earth is a literal spirit child of God, a great preexistent spirit, sent to earth by a loving Father to learn lessons only available through this existence and to learn obedience to His commandments and ordinances, which are necessary for our continued eternal existence in His presence.

No matter what was being taught on the European continent concerning a premortal life after Origen's work was condemned in AD 553, such a concept was apparently part of the doctrines taught to the first Christian converts in England, as shown by the beautiful allegory given in AD 627 by Coifi, the chief Priest of King Edwin, of Northumbria:

> Your Majesty, let us give careful consideration to this new teaching; for I frankly admit that, in my experience, the religion that we have hitherto professed seems valueless and powerless . . .Your Majesty, when we compare the present life of man on earth with that time of which we have no knowledge, it seems to me like the swift flight of a single sparrow through the banqueting-hall where you are sitting at dinner on a winter's day with your thegns and counsellors. In the midst there is a comforting fire to warm the hall; outside, the storms of winter rain or snow are raging. This sparrow flies swiftly in through one door of the hall, and out through another. While he is inside, he is safe from the winter storms; but after a few moments of comfort, he vanishes from sight into the wintry world from which he came. Even so, man appears on earth for a little while; but of what went before this life or of what follows, we know nothing. Therefore, if this new teaching

> has brought any more certain knowledge, it seems only right that we should follow it.[25]

According to this story, the concept of a premortal existence was a key part of the conversion of the English people to Christianity.

Joseph Smith, the Prophet, taught that, "Man was also in the beginning with God. Intelligence, or the light of truth, was not created or made, neither indeed can be."[26] What a wonderful, uplifting perspective on humanity! What a huge difference this belief makes in people's lives compared to the belief that we are some sort of sophisticated marionette, created for God's amusement.

In the April 1844 general conference of the Church, the Prophet Joseph Smith taught the following:

> The mind or the intelligence which man possesses is co-equal with God himself . . .The intelligence of spirits had no beginning, neither will it have an end . . .There never was a time when there were not spirits; for they are co-equal [co-eternal] with our Father in heaven . . .The first principles of man are self-existent with God . . .Intelligence is eternal and exists upon a self-existent principle. It is a spirit from age to age, and there is no creation about it.[27]

The relationship between brain, mind, and intelligence will be discussed in a later chapter. Many early Christians struggled with the notion of how Christ could be co-equal with God the Father and still be His Son. This teaching by the Prophet Joseph Smith moves that entire discussion to an entirely different level, and places human beings in a much higher, eternal environment than most Christians have ever even dreamed of.

Furthermore, we learn from the book of Abraham that,

> Now the Lord had shown unto me, Abraham, the intelligences that were organized before the world was; and among all these there were many of the noble and great ones;
>
> And God saw these souls that they were good, and he stood in the midst of them, and he said: These I will make my rulers; for he stood among those that were spirits,

> and he saw that they were good; and he said unto me: Abraham, thou art one of them; thou wast chosen before thou wast born.[28]

Even though our minds, our intelligences, have existed eternally, we are told that during that infinity before the Grand Council, we were not all the same,

> Howbeit that he made the greater star; as, also, if there be two spirits, and one shall be more intelligent than the other, yet these two spirits, notwithstanding one is more intelligent than the other, have no beginning; they existed before, they shall have no end, they shall exist after, for they are . . . eternal.
>
> And the Lord said unto me: These two facts do exist, that there are two spirits, one being more intelligent than the other; there shall be another more intelligent than they; I am the Lord thy God, I am more intelligent than they all.[29]

This scripture teaches us that it is by the power and level of His intelligence that the Lord is God.

In November 1995, the First Presidency and Quorum of the Twelve Apostles presented "The Family: A Proclamation to the World." A portion of that proclamation states,

> Each is a beloved spirit son or daughter of heavenly parents, and, as such, each has a divine nature and destiny. Gender is an essential characteristic of individual premortal, mortal, and eternal identity and purpose.
>
> In The Premortal Realm, spirit sons and daughters knew and worshiped God as their Eternal Father and accepted His plan by which His children could obtain a physical body and gain earthly experience to progress toward perfection and ultimately realize his or her divine destiny as an heir of eternal life.[30]

This beautiful doctrine of a premortal life was powerfully summarized in 1983 by President Boyd K. Packer, then President of the

Quorum of the Twelve Apostles, “There is no way to make sense out of life without a knowledge of the doctrine of premortal life. . . .When we understand the doctrine of premortal life, then things fit together and make sense.”[31]

---

1. “First Presidency Message,” *Preach My Gospel: A Guide to Missionary Service* (The Church of Jesus Christ of Latter-day Saints, 2019), v.
2. “Nicene Creed,” *Loyola Press,* loyolapress.com/our-catholic-faith/prayer/traditional-catholic-prayers/prayers-every-catholic-should-know/nicene-creed; retrieved 20 Oct. 2019.
3. Ibid.
4. “The Message of the Restoration of the Gospel of Jesus Christ,” *Preach My Gospel: A Guide to Missionary Service* (The Church of Jesus Christ of Latter-day Saints, 2019), 31.
5. “Man, Antemortal Existence of,” *Topical Guide* (The Church of Jesus Christ of Latter-day Saints, 2013), churchofjesuschrist.org/study/scriptures/tg, retrieved 20 Oct. 2019.
6. Job 38:1–7.
7. Ecclesiastes 12:1–7.
8. NASB Lexicon, “Ecclesiastes 12:7,” *Bible Hub*, biblehub.com/lexicon/ecclesiastes/12-7.htm, retrieved 20 Oct. 2019.
9. Psalm 82:6.
10. Givens, Fiona, and Terryl Givens, *The Christ Who Heals* (Salt Lake City, Utah: Deseret Book, 2017), 12.
11. Hebrews 12:9.
12. Acts 17:28–29.
13. Ellicott, Charles, *A New Testament Commentary for English Readers* (New York: Dutton, 1878). Retrieved from “Acts 17:28,” *Bible Hub,* biblehub.com/commentaries/acts/17-28.htm, accessed 22 Oct. 2019.
14. Ibid.
15. Ibid.
16. Acts 17:29.
17. Acts 17:23.
18. Givens, *The Christ Who Heals*, 15.
19. McGuckin, John Anthony, editor, *The Westminster Handbook to Origen* (Louisville, Kentucky: Westminster John Knox Press, 2004), ix.
20. Ibid.
21. Ibid.
22. McGuckin, *The Westminster Handbook to Origen*, x.
23. Laux, John, *Church History, A Complete History of the Catholic Church to the Present Day* (New York, etc,: Benziger Brothers, Inc, 1930), 69.
24. Ibid.
25. Bede, *Ecclesiastical History of the English People, 731 AD*, translated by Leo Sherley-Price (Penguin, 1955, 1990), 130.
26. Doctrine and Covenants 93:29.
27. *Teachings of the Prophet Joseph Smith,* comp. by Joseph Fielding Smith (Salt Lake City, Utah: Deseret Book Co., 1938), 353–54. The bracketed insertion was in the original—the footnote says, “Undoubtedly the proper word here would be ‘co-eternal,’ not ‘co-equal.’ This illustrates the imperfection of the report made of the sermon.” There are four original accounts of the *King Follett* Sermon: Willard Richards used the term “co-equal” in his account; Wilford Woodruff used the term “coequal”; Thomas Bullock said, “man is as immortal as God himself”; William Clayton used the term “coequal”. (See “Discourse, 7 April 1844, as Reported by Willard Richards,” *The Joseph Smith Papers,*

p. 67, accessed 22 Oct. 2019, https://www.josephsmithpapers.org/paper-summary/discourse-7-april-1844-as-reported-by-willard-richards/1).

28. Abraham 3:22–23.
29. Abraham 3:18–19.
30. "The Family: A Proclamation to the World," *Ensign*, Nov. 1995, 102.
31. Packer, Boyd K., "The Mystery of Life," Oct. 1983 general conference.

CHAPTER 3

THE GRAND COUNCIL

As spirit children of our Heavenly Father, we lived with Him in a premortal world where we had our own agency and were able to choose for ourselves. Before the foundation of the world we participated in one or more Grand Councils where the plan of salvation was explained to us and we were able to choose to follow it or not. In the April 2016 general conference, Donald L. Hallstrom, of the Presidency of the Seventy, stated,

> Our most fundamental doctrine includes the knowledge that we are children of a living God. That is why one of his most sacred names is Father—Heavenly Father. . . .[I]t is among the most extraordinary knowledge we can obtain. A correct understanding of our heavenly heritage is essential to exaltation. It is foundational to comprehending the glorious plan of salvation and to nurturing faith in the Firstborn of the Father, Jesus the Christ, and in His merciful atonement.[1]

In the Priesthood session of that same general conference, President Henry B. Eyring, of the First Presidency, stated,

> Before we were born, we lived in a family with our exalted and eternal Heavenly Father. He ordained a plan that enables us to advance and progress to become like

> Him. . . .The purpose of the plan was to allow us the privilege of living forever as our Heavenly Father lives. This gospel plan offered us a life of mortality in which we would be tested. A promise was given that through the Atonement of Jesus Christ, if we obey the laws and priesthood ordinances of the gospel, we would have eternal life, the greatest of all His gifts.[2]

In that premortal state, we lived with two very different kinds of immortal beings. We lived with God the Father who "has a [tangible] body of flesh and bones,"[3] and with Jesus Christ, who had a spirit body just like ours.[4] We could see that God—with His resurrected, tangible, immortal body—was different from us. We were in His exact image but lacked His tangible flesh and bones. When the brother of Jared saw the finger of the premortal Savior, he marveled that it looked like a mortal finger:

> And it came to pass that when the brother of Jared had said these words, behold, the Lord stretched forth his hand and touched the stones one by one with his finger. And the veil was taken from off the eyes of the brother of Jared, and he saw the finger of the Lord; and it was as the finger of a man, like unto flesh and blood; and the brother of Jared fell down before the Lord, for he was struck with fear. . . .
>
> And he saith unto the Lord: I saw the finger of the Lord, and I feared lest he should smite me; for I knew not that the Lord had flesh and blood.
>
> And the Lord said unto him: Because of thy faith thou hast seen that I shall take upon me flesh and blood; and never has man come before me with such exceeding faith as thou hast; for were it not so ye could not have seen my finger. Sawest thou more than this? . . .
>
> Behold, I am he who was prepared from the foundation of the world to redeem my people. Behold, I am Jesus Christ. I am the Father and the Son. In me shall all mankind have life, and that eternally, even they who shall believe on my name; and they shall become my sons and my daughters.[5]

The Brother of Jared was surprised when he saw the finger of Jesus Christ's premortal spirit—"for I knew not that the Lord had flesh and blood." We may assume, from this scripture, that the premortal spirit finger of Christ looked so much like a finger of flesh and blood, that the brother of Jared could not tell the difference. Or, we may believe that Christ was not showing the brother of Jared what He actually looked like, but only what He would look like in the future—"thou hast seen that I shall take upon me flesh and blood."

Whereas this scripture does not specifically clarify between these two alternatives, a scripture in the book of Moses leaves no doubt:

> And I, God, said unto mine Only Begotten, which was with me from the beginning: Let us make man in our image, after our likeness; and it was so. And I, God, said: Let them have dominion over the fishes of the sea, and over the fowl of the air, and over the cattle, and over all the earth, and over every creeping thing that creepeth upon the earth.
>
> And I, God, created man in mine own image, in the image of mine Only Begotten created I him; male and female created I them.[6]

According to this scripture, man was made in "our image . . .in the image of mine Only Begotten." This scripture makes it very clear that the premortal spirit of Jesus Christ was in the express image of the resurrected God the Father. This scripture also makes it clear that *both* propositions for Ether 3 are correct. Taken together, these scriptures reveal that the premortal spirit body of Christ looked *exactly* like His eventual earthly body of flesh and blood, which also looked *exactly* like that of the resurrected Father.[7] Because we were created in the image of the resurrected Father *and* in the image of the premortal spirit Son, we may assume that our premortal spirit body looks exactly like our earthly body of flesh and blood, and they both look exactly like our resurrected immortal body.

As will be discussed in later chapters, the fact that Christ could eat after His resurrection,[8] strongly suggests that His resurrected body was a cellular body—because eating and digesting food is a cellular process. If His spirit body looked exactly like His resurrected body, to the point that the brother of Jared could not tell the difference, then it may be concluded that His, and our, spirit bodies are not some wispy, ethereal, barely perceptible single entity, but are also cellular. The implications this concept advances are enormous and will be discussed more fully in later chapters.

The earth was created to allow us "a life of mortality in which we would be tested."[9] Before the foundation of the world, we attended a Grand Council in Heaven and at least two thirds of us marveled at the great plan of our God[10] and shouted for joy at its prospect.[11] Satan also attended that Council and "came before [God], saying—Behold, here am I, send me, I will be thy son, and I will redeem all mankind, that one soul shall not be lost, and surely I will do it; wherefore give me thine honor."[12] The earth life that God described to us would be a very difficult, frightening experience and many of us may not pass the test and return to His presence. As a result, one third of the host of heaven found Satan's plan of a free ticket back to God's presence too alluring to pass up and, because of their agency, they accepted Satan's proposed plan. Then God's "Beloved, which was my Beloved and Chosen from the beginning, said unto me—Father, thy will be done, and the glory be thine forever."[13] That plan, although it would be difficult and frightening, felt good; it felt right; it was the plan that two thirds of us chose to follow.

With Satan's plan rejected by two thirds of that Grand Premortal Council, he launched a War in Heaven in which one third of heaven's host was drawn away with him, away from God's presence: "And there was war in heaven: Michael and his angels fought against the dragon; and the dragon fought and his angels."[14] "And his tail drew the third part of the stars of heaven, and did cast them to the earth."[15] This story is confirmed by modern revelation: "[T]he devil . . .rebelled against me, saying, Give me thine honor, which is my power; and also a third part of the hosts of heaven turned he away from me because of their agency."[16]

All of us who accepted the Savior's plan were foreordained to accept Jesus Christ as our Savior here on earth:

> And we know that all things work together for good to them that love God, to them who are the called according to his purpose. For whom he did foreknow, he also did

> predestinate to be conformed to the image of his Son, that he might be the firstborn among many brethren. Moreover whom he did predestinate, them he also called: and whom he called, them he also justified: and whom he justified, them he also glorified.[17]

> According as he hath chosen us in him before the foundation of the world, that we should be holy and without blame before him in love.[18]

In addition, all of us who hold the priesthood and/or have specific callings in the Church were foreordained to the priesthood and to those callings before we came to earth—this includes all those who accept the priesthood and its ordinances in the spirit world after their earthly lives are finished.

> And those priests were ordained after the order of his Son . . .being called and prepared from the foundation of the world according to the foreknowledge of God, on account of their exceeding faith and good works;[19]

> Before I formed thee in the belly I knew thee; and before thou camest forth out of the womb I sanctified thee, and I ordained thee a prophet unto the nations.[20]

> And God saw these souls that they were good, and he stood in the midst of them, and he said: These I will make my rulers; for he stood among those that were spirits, and he saw that they were good; and he said unto me: Abraham, thou art one of them; thou wast chosen before thou wast born.[21]

Although not discussed in the scriptures, as part of our premortal education, we must have been taught of Adam and Eve's roles in the great plan of salvation. Because without a knowledge of the Fall, the Atonement of Jesus Christ would make no sense. How could we know that Jesus Christ would overcome the death introduced into the world by Adam if we knew nothing of Adam's transgression?

Adam was Michael, whom we all knew very well in our premortal life.[22] He was the Archangel, our great leader, our captain in our struggle against Satan and his minions.[23] According to Merriam-Webster, an archangel is "a chief angel."[24] In Adam's case, he was *the* chief angel. According to the online thesaurus, chief also means: leading, main, preeminent, prime, principle, or first.[25] In other words, Michael, was numero uno among all the premortal angels: all of us sons and daughters of God. When Michael came to earth as Adam, he retained that title of "First," and was called the first man, the first flesh also.[26] This was no chronological designation, as there is no chronology with God,[27] but rather, that *title* was a continuation of his designation as the first, the preeminent of God's angelic children, second only to Jesus Christ.

---

1. Hallstrom, Donald L., "I *Am* a Child of God," Apr. 2016 general conference.
2. Eyring, Henry B., "Eternal Families," Apr. 2016 general conference.
3. Doctrine and Covenants 130:22.
4. Abraham 3:18–23.
5. Ether 3:6, 8–9, 14.
6. Moses 2:26–27.
7. See John 14:7–9.
8. Luke 24:39–43.
9. Eyring, Henry B., "Eternal Families," Apr. 2016 general conference.
10. 2 Nephi 9:13.
11. Job 38:7.
12. Moses 4:1.
13. Moses 4:2.
14. Revelation 12:7.
15. Revelation 12:4.
16. Doctrine and Covenants 29:36.
17. Romans 8:28–30.
18. Ephesians 1:4.
19. Alma 13:2–3.
20. Jeremiah 1:5.
21. Abraham 3:22.
22. Revelation 12:7.
23. Doctrine and Covenants 107:54.
24. "Archangel," *Merriam-Webster Dictionary,* merriam-webster.com/dictionary/archangel, retrieved 11 Dec. 2019.
25. "Chief," *Thesaurus.com,* thesaurus.com/browse/chief, retrieved 11 Dec. 2019.
26. Moses 3:7.
27. Alma 40:8.

CHAPTER 4

THE VIRGIN BIRTH PARADOX

What makes us human, what made Jesus Christ human, was only vaguely understood before 1900. Over one hundred years later, it is difficult for us to appreciate just how little information was available previously and how much room there was for "mystery." Although the Austrian monk Gregor Mendel discovered the basic principles of inheritance in 1865–1866, his data remained largely unknown and certainly unappreciated until 1900, when Carl Correns, Hugo de Vries, and Erich von Tschermak, independently, rediscovered Mendel's paper and confirmed his findings.[1] Then in 1902–1904, Walter Sutton and Theodor Boveri, independently, published papers connecting Mendel's concept that two genes code for a characteristic to the idea that cells contain two sets of chromosomes.[2]

In 1915, Thomas Hunt Morgan stated that, "It is difficult to resist the fascinating assumption that the gene is constant because it represents an organic chemical entity."[3] It's hard for us to imagine, one hundred years later, that this concept of genes being organic chemical entities was somewhat revolutionary. About the same time, biologists specializing in cell structure (cytologists) began to propose that sex was determined by odd chromosomes, called X and Y. Morgan discovered that several Mendelian traits were "linked" to the same chromosome.[4] He, with three of his students, Sturtevant, Muller, and Bridges, published a groundbreaking book, *The Mechanism of Mendelian Heredity*, which clearly demonstrated that genes were located on chromosomes and revolutionized the concepts of heredity.[5]

Nearly forty years later, on 25 April 1953, James Watson and Francis Crick elucidated the structure of deoxyribonucleic acid (DNA) and demonstrated the "organic chemical" basis of genetics.[6] Then in 1956, Joe Hin Tjio and Albert Levan established the correct number of chromosomes in humans to be 46.[7] Completion of the human genome project, which was announced 25 April 2003, exactly 50 years after Watson and Crick's paper, informed us that we have approximately 20,000 genes, which make us human.[8] Since then, April 25th has been designated International DNA Day—there should be parades.

We now know that humans have approximately 20,000 genes located on 46 chromosomes, two of which—"X" and "Y"—determine sex. We, therefore, can also conclude that Jesus Christ, being a male human, had 20,000 genes on 46 chromosomes, with an "X" chromosome from his mother, Mary, a virgin, and a "Y" chromosome from his father, God. For most Christians, this is the paradox: how did a virgin give birth to a child? Not for me. For me, the paradox is much further upstream in the thought process.

It seems that nearly every Christmas season some critic comes out with an essay or letter to the editor pointing out how dumb Christians are for believing in a virgin birth. As an example, on 18 November 2013, Daniel Engber, a journalist who likes to write about "weird news" in science and culture for the *New York Times Magazine*, *Slate*, *Wired*, and *Popular Science*, among others, came out with such a story in his *Popular Science* column. His heading: "Could A Virgin Birth Ever Happen?" His short answer: "If you're a mammal, no." Engber stated concerning a virgin birth, "Virgin birth, known to scientists as parthenogenesis, appears to be rather common in the animal kingdom. . . . But humans and our fellow mammals provide a notable exception."[9]

Apparently, Engber did not grow up on a farm, around animals, and believes that the only type of virgin birth to occur is by parthenogenesis—reproduction from an egg only, with no sperm involved. Whereas everything Engber said about the barriers to mammalian parthenogenesis is correct, he missed the most important point concerning Christ's birth: any mammal developed parthenogenetically would be *female.* I have often stressed this point in my nearly forty years of teaching developmental biology and human embryology. Parthenogenesis, however, is not the only type of virgin birth available.

I grew up on a dairy farm where we milked about seventy-five cows twice a day. No adult bull ever set foot on our farm, yet, each spring, our cows delivered about seventy-five calves—all by artificial insemination—all born to virgin cows. According to Merriam-Webster, a virgin is "a female animal that has never copulated," i.e. never engaged "in sexual intercourse." By definition, every one of our cows was a virgin, yet each produced a calf by virgin birth roughly annually. For me, growing up on a dairy farm, it's not at all difficult to believe in a virgin birth. For humans, Merriam-Webster also defines a virgin as "a person who has not had sexual intercourse." Therefore, by definition, Mary gave birth to the Savior without ever having had sexual intercourse. Currently, artificial insemination is fairly common in humans, occurring as many as 50,000 times per year.[10] Mary contributed 23 chromosomes, one of which was an "X" chromosome, toward her son. The other 23 chromosomes, including the "Y" chromosome, came from Jesus's father—God. Because we believe that Mary was a virgin, we do not believe that this occurred through sexual intercourse—but that is not the only way 23 chromosomes from a male can combine with the 23 female chromosomes. If we, as mere mortals, can figure out how to produce offspring in virgins, it is, in our modern society, not at all difficult to believe that God could also accomplish such a feat.

We do know, however, that the 23 female chromosomes and 23 male chromosomes have to be compatible and able to pair up very closely in order for mitosis (a critical part of cell division) to occur in the developing embryo, the next human being. The implication here is that God, being the biological father of Jesus Christ, contributed 23 chromosomes that were enough compatible with Mary's 23 chromosomes for mitosis to occur in Jesus's cells.

I don't believe that God was the father of Jesus Christ by some hocus pocus magic, mystical bologna—in a similar way to Geppetto's being Pinocchio's father. Herein lies the paradox, how did God contribute exactly 23 chromosomes, including a "Y" chromosome, that were compatible with Mary's 23 chromosomes and 20,000 genes, which apparently developed at random through the process of evolution?

This is the true virgin birth paradox. That paradox, which elevates the discussion to a whole new level—that of quantum genetics, will take more time to work through and will, of necessity, be a topic for another book. However, the topic is briefly discussed in the next chapter.

Isaiah prophesied of the virgin birth of the Savior. "Therefore the Lord himself shall give you a sign; Behold, a virgin shall conceive, and bear a son, and shall call his name Immanuel."[11]

Several scholars, however, have attempted to humanize the Son of God by proposing that the word "virgin" in the King James version of Isaiah is a mistranslation. For example, Joel Hoffman—who calls himself an independent scholar, teacher, translator, and author—stated the following,

> But he [Matthew] is quoting a mistranslation. The original Hebrew text of Isa 7:14 is not about a virgin. Rather, the Hebrew used to describe the woman in Isa 7:14 is *almah,* a word that means "young woman." But then the Septuagint, an early translation of the Hebrew Bible into Greek, took the Hebrew *almah* and rendered it as the Greek *parthenos,* which means "virgin."[12]

Hoffman goes on to state,

> In most contexts, calling a "young woman" a "virgin" in the days of the Septuagint would be only a minor translation mistake, hardly even noteworthy, because most young women were virgins, and most female virgins were young women. In modern terms, it would be like mixing up "high schooler" and "teenager"—imprecise perhaps, but good enough for most purposes.
>
> But in one situation, obviously, turning a young woman into a virgin rises to the level of a serious gaffe. And that's when the young woman is pregnant. This is how the Septuagint, through lack of precision, turned an ordinary birth into a virgin birth.[13]

Such an explanation may satisfy a skeptical world but has no footing in a believing world. Hoffman's statement that a young woman was usually a virgin is on point in Mary's case.

By contrast, Nephi's prophecy in the Book of Mormon, a second testimony of Christ's divinity, makes it very clear that Jesus's birth was no *ordinary* birth.

> And it came to pass that I looked and beheld the great city of Jerusalem, and also other cities. And I beheld the city of Nazareth; and in the city of Nazareth I beheld a virgin, and she was exceedingly fair and white. . . .
>
> And he [the angel] said unto me: Behold, the virgin whom thou seest is the mother of the Son of God, after the manner of the flesh. And it came to pass that I beheld that she was carried away in the Spirit; and after she had been carried away in the Spirit for the space of a time the angel spake unto me, saying: Look! And I looked and beheld the virgin again, bearing a child in her arms.[14]

The books of Mark and John, in the New Testament, begin with Christ's baptism and focus on His ministry, except that the first five verses in John describe Christ as the creator of "All things."[15] Some scholars have made an issue of the fact that Mark and John exclude Christ's virgin birth. This seems to me to follow the same question I will address in other chapters; for example: why did only Matthew mention the star, why are most miracles only mentioned in one gospel, and why did John alone mention Lazarus? This issue of not all the gospels mentioning the virgin birth appears to come mostly from Jewish scholars who wish to undermine the divinity of Christ and from Catholic and other Christian scholars who put an undue emphasis on His virgin birth—teaching that Mary was not only a virgin at the time of Christ's birth but remained so throughout her life—and denying the scriptures stating that Christ had brothers and sisters, in spite of what we read:

> While he yet talked to the people, behold, his mother and his brethren stood without, desiring to speak with him. Then one said unto him, Behold, thy mother and thy brethren stand without, desiring to speak with thee.[16]

The real-life, human, forty-six-chromosome-twenty-thousand-gene nature of Christ is emphasized in Mark's gospel, when His neighbors inquired, "Is not this the carpenter, the son of Mary, the brother of James, and Joses, and of Juda, and Simon? and are not his sisters here with us? And they were offended at him."[17]

Historically, for most of the time since Jesus lived, people could believe that Christ was human by some magical sleight of hand, much like the Blue Fairy turning the wooden Pinocchio into a real boy, or the magician Drosselmeyer turning Chikaskia's Nutcracker into a real prince. Today, however, with our understanding of cells and chromosomes and genes, those age-old fairytales remain just that.

Under the heading, "Mary the Blessed Virgin," we are told by the Catholic Online that,

"Traditionally, she [Mary] was declared the daughter of Sts. Joachim and Anne. Born in Jerusalem, Mary was presented in the Temple and took a vow of virginity." There is not a single scriptural reference to support this Catholic tradition. Then we are told that, "The four Catholic dogmas are: Mother of God, Perpetual virginity of Mary, the Immaculate Conception and Assumption of Mary.[18]

Catholics and other Christians often attempt to argue away Matthew 12:46–47 and Mark 6:3 by saying that they were Joseph's children by a previous marriage—or some other, similar argument.[19]

In *The Oxford Dictionary of the Christian Church* we are told that those who hold to the notion of the perpetual virginity of Mary, reject the idea that Jesus had biological siblings and maintain that those designated as brothers and sisters were actually either cousins or children of Joseph by a previous marriage.[20]

For the vast majority of Christians, then, Mary's perpetual virginity is in some way critical to their whole belief system. The concept of the *Trinity* further complicates the very idea of a virgin birth for Jesus (the origin of the trinitarian concept will be discussed in later chapters). How could Christ be His own father and how could a bodiless, formless entity be a father at all? How could God, who is an "immaterial spirit who has an entirely simple . . . nature—that is, a nature containing no parts,"[21] contribute twenty-three chromosomes and 20,000 genes toward a son that is somehow Himself? The answer—it's a *miracle*, it's a *mystery*.

I believe in miracles, but I believe that they all occur by obedience to a higher law as yet unknown to the observers. A miracle is explaining to someone from Christ's time how seventy-five cows became pregnant with no bull present. A miracle is a person living a hundred years ago being told that there are humans with artificial hearts or organ transplants. To that person, who does not understand the application of higher laws—unknown in their time—artificial hearts and transplanted organs would appear miraculous. The term *mystery*, on the other hand, is simply a convenient way of saying, "Don't ask because no one can explain it." With such attitudes in modern churches, it is little wonder that the younger generation is leaving Christianity in large numbers. Unfortunately, because many young people who are members of The Church of Jesus Christ of Latter-day Saints don't appreciate that we are not those Christians, they are being caught up in the general exodus. Because most churches, unfortunately sometimes including ours, don't even attempt to bring science to bare on these "mysteries," being Christian is seen by many Millennials as not cool.

---

1. Mukherjee, Siddartha, *The Gene: An Intimate History* (New York, New York: Scribner, 2016).
2. Sutton, WS, "On the morphology of the chromosome group," *Brachystola magna. Biol Bull* (1902), 4:24–39; Sutton, WS, "The chromosomes in heredity," *Biol Bull* (1903), 4:231–251; Boveri, Theodor, *Ergebnisse über die Konstitution der chromatischen Substanz des Zellkerns*, (Fisher in Jena, 1904).
3. Shine, Ian and Sylvia Wrobel, *Thomas Hunt Morgan, Pioneer of Genetics* (Lexington, KY: University Press of Kentucky, 1976).
4. Ibid.
5. Morgan, TH, AH Sturtevant, HJ Muller, and CB Bridges, *The Mechanism of Mendelian Heredity* (New York, New York: Henry Holt, 1915).
6. Watson, JD and FHC Crick, "A Structure for Deoxyribose Nucleic Acid," *Nature* 171 (1953), 737–38.
7. Tjio, JH and A Levan, "The chromosome number of man," *Hereditas* (1956), 42:1–6.
8. International Human Genome Sequencing Consortium, "Finishing the euchromatic sequence of the human genome," *Nature* (2004), 431: 931–945.
9. Engber, Daniel, "FYI: Could A Virgin Birth Ever Happen?," *Popular Science*, 18 Nov. 2013, popsci.com/article/science/fyi-could-virgin-birth-ever-happen.
10. Yadegaran, Jessica, "No Mr. Right? More women start families via artificial insemination," *Mercury News*, 13 Aug. 2010. This is an estimate, because the fertility industry is not required to report on these statistics.
11. Isaiah 7:14.
12. Hoffman, Joel W., "Was There Really a Virgin Birth in the Bible?", bibleodyssey.com; Adapted from Hoffman, Joel W., *And God Said: How Translations Conceal the Bible's Original Meaning* (St. Martin's Press, 2010), ch. 8.
13. Ibid.
14. 1 Nephi 11:13, 18–20.
15. John 1:3.

16. Matthew 12:46–47; see also Mark 3:31 and Galatians 1:19.
17. Mark 6:3.
18. "Mary the Blessed Virgin," *Catholic Online*, catholic.org/saints/saint.php?saint_id=4967.
19. Ibid.
20. Cross, Frank Leslie, and Livingstone, Elizabeth A., "Brethren of the Lord," *The Oxford Dictionary of the Christian Church*, Oxford University Press, 2005.
21. "What the Early Church Believed: God Has No Body," *Catholic Answers*, catholic.com/tract/god-has-no-body, retrieved 12 Dec. 2019.

CHAPTER 5

THE PINOCCHIO SYNDROME

I didn't like Pinocchio when I was a child. I don't recall the first time I saw the Walt Disney movie—it was produced in 1940, eight years before I was born—but however young I was, I didn't like it. I will admit that he had a cute face, but to me that only belied the dark side of his personality. First of all, I didn't like marionettes—I thought they were freaky—and besides, any time I tried to make one work, I just got the strings all tangled up. Beyond that, I didn't like Pinocchio's wooden-headed blundering into trouble, and most of all, I was never convinced that a wooden puppet could ever become a real boy. I did like Jiminy Cricket. Now that's a character I could relate to. I also liked Geppetto. I always wanted to have a shop where I could make wooden toys. I actually have accomplished that dream in part. I have made dozens of toy castles and even have a website called build-modelcastles.com.

According to *The Adventures of Pinocchio*, by Carlo Collodi (1883), Pinocchio started life as an animated block of wood "that wept and laughed like a child,"[1] but according to Walt Disney's *Pinocchio* (1940), a Blue Fairy made Pinocchio magically come alive, and promised him that he could become a real child if he could "prove himself to be brave, truthful, and unselfish and able to tell right from wrong by listening to his conscience."[2]

The days of believing in Pinocchio are past. Science has progressed beyond beliefs in puppets or blocks of wood that can come to life. As Paul said, "When I was a child . . . I thought as a child: but when I became a man, I put away childish things."[3] We read in the Gospel of Matthew:

> And it came to pass, that when Jesus had finished these parables, he departed thence. And when he was come into his own country, he taught them in their synagogue, insomuch that they were astonished, and said, Whence hath this man this wisdom, and these mighty works? Is not this the carpenter's son? is not his mother called Mary? and his brethren, James, and Joses, and Simon, and Judas? And his sisters, are they not all with us? Whence then hath this man all these things? And they were offended in him. But Jesus said unto them, A prophet is not without honour, save in his own country, and in his own house. And he did not many mighty works there because of their unbelief.[4]

Few people doubt that a real, physical person named Jesus Christ actually lived. What is debated is the physical nature of that person, Jesus. The central tenant of Christian belief is that Jesus Christ is the physical, begotten Son of God. For nearly two thousand years, it was possible for people to believe that in some foggy, mystical, mysterious, nebulous way Christ was the Son of God, much like Pinocchio was the son of Geppetto, but such a belief cannot stand by itself in the light of the 21st century. I would like to go back in time and have Pinocchio spit into a bottle so I could have his DNA tested and see where he really came from. Even better, I would like to obtain a sample of Christ's "true blood" from one of the many relics collectors and have its DNA tested.

The latter project is actually not as hard as it sounds. As the story goes, it turns out that there is a vial containing a cloth with Christ's blood on it in the Basilica of the Holy Blood in Bruges, Belgium. The blood was allegedly originally collected by no less than Joseph of Arimathea and was brought to Belgium from the Holy Land by Thierry of Alsace, Count of Flanders around 1150. The count built a private chapel between 1134 and 1157 which housed the relic, and the chapel was later designated a minor basilica. Thierry had made several trips to the Holy Land, including a trip to Jerusalem in 1139, where he married Sibylla of Anjou, daughter of King Fulk of Jerusalem, and, later, as a leader in the Second Crusade in 1147. It was apparently during the Second Crusade trip that Thierry obtained the blood-soaked cloth, but its provenance after Joseph of Arimathea supposedly collected it in approximately AD 33 is unclear.[5]

It is not at all clear what happened to the cloth and blood after AD 33 or how Thierry took possession of it. I have my own theory: Apparently, bazaars were common in the early Middle Ages in the Middle East and throughout Europe, where you could buy anything you could possibly imagine, and then some. And at that time, in those markets, relics were hot items. Splinters from the original cross, called the Holy Rood, were commonly available; thorns from the original Crown of Thorns were probably a dime a dozen. There were enough apostles' and martyrs' bones for sale to build an army, and there were apparently numerous vials of Jesus blood. The relic stands were run by local merchants of Middle Eastern heritage who were certainly not above taking advantage of a gullible Christian pilgrim.

It turns out that, today, the world's largest public collection of relics, over 5,000 total, is on display in St. Anthony's Chapel in, believe it or not, Pittsburgh, Pennsylvania, USA. The largest *private* collection is in the Vatican, as might be expected. How did a church in Pittsburgh, of all places, end up with the world's largest public relic collection? According to the Team at Roadside America, it was Father Suitbert Godfrey Mollinger:

> Father Mollinger was the pastor of Most Holy Name Parish, an inconsequential congregation in what was then the boondocks north of Pittsburgh. He also turned out to be the greatest collector of Catholic relics in history. Born and raised in Belgium, from a wealthy noble family, he had credibility, connections, and money—and he used them to acquire thousands of relics from churches and monasteries in the politically chaotic Europe of the mid-1800s. "He rescued them," said Carole of the relics. "Most of them would have been destroyed."[6]

The St. Anthony's relic collection includes skulls from several saints. (As an anatomist visiting cathedrals in Europe, I have been often intrigued by a number of statues I passed either holding actual human skulls or having skulls at their feet.) The Chapel has on display the complete skeleton of St. Demetrius (one of several saints by the same name). It also exhibits a reliquary displaying bone chips from *each* of the Apostles—"not an easy collection to assemble." There is a fragment of Mary's veil and a thorn from the Crown of Thorns. There are two splinters of wood from the table used at the Last Supper and no less than twenty-two separate pieces of the Holy Rood, splinters from the original cross. And, oh yes, one of St Anthony's teeth.[7]

There is one slight catch in obtaining a sample of Jesus's blood. The phial containing the blood, in the Basilica of the Holy Blood in Bruges, was originally a Byzantine perfume bottle, made in Constantinople, of rock crystal dating from the 11th or 12th century. The phial has never been opened since its arrival in Bruges nearly nine hundred years ago. The stopper is sealed with red wax and the neck of the phial is wrapped with gold thread. The phial is encased in a glass cylinder closed at each end with a gold crown.[8] It would take a Dan Brown or Jim Kouf-like adventure to enter the basilica, open the glass cylinder, remove the stopper from the phial, snip off a sample of blood-soaked cloth, replace all the items, and escape without being detected and decapitated—this sounds like the stuff of a future adventure book/movie.

Nonetheless, let's suppose we *could* obtain a DNA sample from Christ, which we send along to AncestryDNA or 23andMe. What would we find? His mitochondrial DNA (mDNA), which provides the mother's bloodline, would show a middle eastern origin from around AD 0, and would match that of His mother Mary. Although Luke 3:23–38 is often cited as Jesus's linage through Mary, the scriptures say nothing about her parents. Tradition and apocryphal writings list her parents as Joachim and Anne.[9] Beyond Anne, there is no maternal lineage for Christ listed anywhere.

We next consider Christ's paternal line. The genealogy presented in Mathew 1:1–16 is that of Joseph, Jesus's adopted father, not His biological father. There is no pedigree listed anywhere for *that* Father. What we can say about Jesus's biological Father is that He "has a body of flesh and bones as tangible as man's."[10] The fact that Jesus Christ was a living, breathing human male also tells us that His Father has cells with 46 chromosomes, including a "Y" chromosome—as discussed in the previous chapter. If this were not the case, God would be no more Jesus's actual biological father than Geppetto was Pinocchio's.

The problem for most Christians is the *Trinity*, a concept that was institutionalized at the council of Nicaea, as will be discussed in more detail in a later chapter. After AD 325, anyone believing that the Godhead consisted of three separate beings was branded a heretic. The Emperor Constantine exiled the first Arian heretics—those who had stood up for the idea of three separate individuals—in opposition to Constantine's wishes. Later heretics—in the thousands—were burned at the stake. Today, the Nicene Creed states,

> We believe in one God, the Father almighty, maker of heaven and earth, of all things visible and invisible. And in one Lord Jesus Christ, the only Son of God, begotten from the Father before all ages, God from God, Light from Light, true God from true God, begotten, not made; of the same essence as the Father.[11]

The associated problem with the Trinity is the belief that God is spirit and was only incarnated in the form of Jesus Christ. Thus, in some mysterious way, Christ became His own son. The Catholic Catechism (point 461) states, "Taking up St. John's expression, 'The Word became flesh,' the Church calls 'Incarnation' the fact that the Son of God assumed a human nature in order to accomplish our salvation in it."[12]

An integral part of the *Trinity* is, according to the Catechism,

> Belief in the true Incarnation of the Son of God is the distinctive sign of Christian faith: "By this you know the Spirit of God: every spirit which confesses that Jesus Christ has come in the flesh is of God." Such is the joyous conviction of the Church from her beginning whenever she sings "the mystery of our religion": "He was manifested in the flesh."[13]

Before the incarnation of Jesus, the Trinity doctrine argues that God was *only* spirit, citing Jesus's statement in John, "God *is* a Spirit: and they that worship him must worship him in spirit and in truth."[14]

It turns out that, according to the King James Version of the Bible, the word "is" in John 4:24 [shown in italics] was added by the translators and was not there in the original. Thus the original phrase was: "God a Spirit," with the verb missing. As English does not work without verbs, the King James translators added the verb "is." The Darby Bible Translation states, "God [is] a spirit," emphasizing that "is" was an added term. I make this point to emphasize the ambiguity of the phrase. Why didn't the translators add the verb "has" instead? For one reason—because in 1611 they were already steeped in trinitarian philosophy. Despite the word "is" not being in the original text, nearly all Christians believe that "God is a spirit." The Catholic Answers website goes even farther, declaring that John 4:24 states that, "God is spirit."[15] They have removed the "a" which was there in the original and retained only the "is," which was not there but was added de novo by the translators.

Members of The Church of Jesus Christ of Latter-day Saints are unique among Christians in that we believe in a God who has a spirit, but who also has a body of flesh and bones as tangible as man's, as witnessed by the Prophet Joseph Smith.[16] In February 1832, the Prophet Joseph Smith and Sidney Rigdon bore joint testimony:

> And now, after the many testimonies which have been given of him, this is the testimony, last of all, which we give of him: That he lives! For we saw him, even on the right hand of God; and we heard the voice bearing record that he is the Only Begotten of the Father—That by him, and through him, and of him, the worlds are and were created, and the inhabitants thereof are begotten sons and daughters unto God.[17]

Then in March of the same year, the prophet Joseph received additional revelation:

> Q. What are we to understand by the four beasts, spoken of in the same verse? [Revelation 4:6]
>
> A. They are figurative expressions, used by the Revelator, John, in describing heaven, the paradise of God, the happiness of man, and of beasts, and of creeping things, and of the fowls of the air; that which is spiritual being in the likeness of that which is temporal; and that which is

> temporal in the likeness of that which is spiritual; the spirit of man in the likeness of his person, as also the spirit of the beast, and every other creature which God has created.[18]

We are further informed in Moses chapter 2: "And I, God, said unto mine Only Begotten, which was with me from the beginning: Let us make man in our image, after our likeness; and it was so."[19]

In 1843, the Prophet Joseph Smith revealed that, "There is no such thing as immaterial matter. All spirit is matter, but it is more fine or pure, and can only be discerned by purer eyes; We cannot see it; but when our bodies are purified we shall see that it is all matter."[20]

We know, therefore, by revelation that we are "begotten sons and daughters unto God," that "the spirit of man [is] in the likeness of his person," that we were created in the likeness of the Father and the Son, and that our spirits are made of pure, fine matter. The fact that God our Father has a cellular body with the same genes and chromosomes as we have—as evidenced by His being the earthly father of Jesus Christ, argues that our spirit bodies are cellular, with chromosomes, and genes—weird as this may seem.

The grand paradox of science and scripture is this: how are we in the express image of God, right down to the cellular and genetic level, and yet are the products of random mutation and evolution? The answer to this paradox is certainly not readily apparent, but a solution may be emerging from the strangest branch of science we know: quantum entanglement.

God told Isaiah, "For my thoughts are not your thoughts, neither are your ways my ways, saith the Lord. For as the heavens are higher than the earth, so are my ways higher than your ways, and my thoughts than your thoughts."[21]

Is it possible that God was referring to the mysterious notion of entanglement when He made that statement—one of the most bazar concepts to ever emerge from scientific investigation? Albert Einstein might say yes. He referred to entanglement as "spooky action at a distance." In 1935, Einstein, Boris Podolsky, and Nathan Rosen published a paper describing a thought experiment concerning the quantum mechanics of strongly correlated systems. Through their research, they discovered that such systems behave in ways that are not predicted by any existing laws of physics, even of quantum physics. They stated, "We are thus forced to conclude that the quantum-mechanical description of physical reality given by wave functions is not complete." This pronouncement has become known as the Einstein, Podolsky, Rosen paradox, or simply the EPR paradox.[22]

Even though Einstein, Podolsky, and Rosen described the phenomenon they had discovered, they did not give it a name. Erwin Schrödinger, another major player in the new field of quantum theory, wrote a letter to Einstein shortly after the EPR paradox paper was published, and used the term "entanglement" to describe "the correlations between two particles that interact and then separate, as in the EPR experiment." Shortly thereafter, still in 1935, Schrödinger published his own paper expanding upon the EPR concepts and calling this new interaction entanglement. Quantum entanglement is defined as "a physical phenomenon that occurs when pairs or groups of particles are generated or interact in ways such that the quantum state of each particle cannot be described independently of the others, even when the particles are separated by a large distance." Schrödinger stated, "I would not call [entanglement] *one* but rather *the* characteristic trait of quantum mechanics, the one that enforces its entire departure from classical lines of thought."[23]

Here are two colloquial examples to help explain quantum entanglement: First, consider the flip of a coin—a term we even use to exemplify randomness. When we flip a coin, the outcome—heads or tails—is believed to be unaffected by any considerations, such as what we want the coin to do or what happened the last time it was flipped. That is true as long as the coins are not entangled. If they are entangled, however, the flip of one coin will always determine the outcome of the other, entangled coin flip. If one coin comes up heads, then so will the other coin—always—even across great distances, such as across the width of the galaxy. If the coins are inversely entangled, the second coin will always come up tails when the first coin is heads. That's why Einstein called such a connection "spooky action at a distance." Einstein had a hard time believing what he had discovered and spent much of the rest of his life trying to disprove it—but entanglement has stood the test of time for over eighty years and has stood up to test after test.

The second colloquial example is as follows: Say you leave home for work and when you arrive there, you discover you have only one glove, but you have not as yet checked to see which glove it is. There is a 50:50 chance it is the left glove, exactly the probability of a coin flip. There is also a 50:50 chance that the glove you left home is the left glove. Then you reach into your pocket and discover that the glove you have with you is the right glove. The probability now becomes 100% that the glove you have is the right glove, but, even more importantly, there is now also a 100% chance that the glove at home is the left glove.[24]

In a 2016 paper in *Nature Physics*, Kaspar Sakmann and Mark Kasevich, from the Department of Physics, Stanford University, discovered that in an ultracold cloud of bosons (a subatomic class of particles, including photons; the cloud is called a Bose-Einstein condensate and was used in the EPR experiment), the bosons become entangled such that random fluctuations in one element of the system can affect other elements of the system in ways "driven by information beyond what is typically available in low-order correlation functions."[25]

In application to general physics and chemistry, the Sakmann-Kasevich experiment suggests that a Bose-Einstein condensate is acting like a crystal. Expanding upon this theorem, we may conclude that ions in a chemical crystal, such as the sodium and chloride ions in a salt crystal, may be considered to be "entangled," with a predictable, structural relationship between the ions such that knowing the position of one ion determines the positions of the others. Such crystalline entanglement extends all the way to DNA.[26] The secret to DNA structure—the whole basis of inheritance, which had remained hidden for millions of years, is that the two halves of the DNA double helix are "entangled" so that the sequence of nucleotides in one half of the double helix determines the *exact* sequence of nucleotides in the other half: based on their exact chemical structure.

The DNA sequence in our 20,000 genes, however, appears to be relatively random. Herein lies a paradox that requires solution. Is there any way that the random DNA sequence in the human genome can in some way be determinate rather than purely stochastic?

About seven years ago, William Poirier, Professor of Chemistry and Biochemistry, and Joint Professor of Physics at Texas Tech University was researching the quantum mechanics of complex molecules. His research led him, and us, into a strange new parallel universe that may be "poking through into our own." In his research, Poirier "found a completely new way to draw quantum landscapes. Instead of waves, his medium became parallel universes."[27] Poirier's theory has become known as "Many Interacting Worlds." John Davis made the following comment about this theory,

> In his theory, Poirier postulates that small particles from many worlds seep through to interact with our own, and their interaction accounts for the strange phenomena of quantum mechanics. Such phenomena include particles that seem to be in more than one place at a time, or to communicate with each other over great distances without explanations. . . . Likewise, quantum communication of faraway particles [entanglement] . . . is actually due to interaction of nearby worlds.[28]

Davis quoted Poirier as stating,

> We don't have proof that an alternate me or you might be president [sic: present?]. I can't say whether those worlds exist or not. According to the theory, the only worlds we can directly interact with are so close to our own world that we hardly can tell them apart, except at the quantum scale. . . .[T]hat doesn't rule out the possibility that there are indeed more distant worlds macroscopically different from our own where you and I are living out any number of counterfactual existences. We don't have any direct evidence for that. But then again, nor should we, according to the theory, even if such worlds do exist.[29]

Let's go back and consider the spiritual implications of Poirier's proposals. "Poirier postulates that small particles from many worlds seep through to interact with our own . . .'so close to our own world that we hardly can tell them apart.'"[30] What if those "small particles" from other worlds, so near to us, might be called spirit matter?

Then, in 2016, Juan Maldacena, a theoretical physicist at the Institute for Advanced Study, Princeton, filled in some more of the picture: "[S]peculate that the link is more general—that whenever we have entanglement we have a kind of geometric connection [a crystal]. . . .When the amount of entanglement becomes larger, we have lots of threads, and these threads could weave together to form the fabric of spacetime."[31] With lots and lots of threads, indeed billions, our spirit selves and our physical selves may be so entangled that they match right down to the subatomic level. Now this is some exciting stuff—stuff that even Millennials can get their teeth into.

Is it, therefore, possible that our spirit bodies are so entangled with our physical bodies that the determinism of the former can drive the stochastic evolution of the latter? Is it possible that what we perceive as a totally random process, evolution, as in the case of entangled coins, can be determined by our entangled spirits? Is it possible that we participated in our own creation? We are told, after all,

> Thus the heaven and the earth were finished, and all the host of them.
>
> And on the seventh day I, God, ended my work, and all things which I had made; and I rested on the seventh day from all my work, and all things which I had made were finished, and I, God, saw that they were good;
>
> And I, God, blessed the seventh day, and sanctified it; because that in it I had rested from all my work which I, God, had created and made.
>
> And now, behold, I say unto you, that these are the generations of the heaven and of the earth, when they were created, in the day that I, the Lord God, made the heaven and the earth,
>
> And every plant of the field before it was in the earth, and every herb of the field before it grew. For I, the Lord God, created all things, of which I have spoken, spiritually, before they were naturally upon the face of the earth. For I, the Lord God, had not caused it to rain upon the face of the earth. And I, the Lord God, had created all the children of men; and not yet a man to till the ground; for in heaven created I them; and there was not yet flesh upon the earth, neither in the water, neither in the air.[32]

Is it possible that the evolutionary processes we perceive here on earth actually occurred in a parallel, spirit universe? We are not talking about science fiction here; we have way outstripped science fiction. But these are ideas suggested by scientific research published in leading scientific journals in the past few years. I think it's safe to say, "We are no longer in Kansas, Toto."

---

1. Collodi, Carlo, *The Adventures of Pinocchio* (1883), Sterling Children's Books Unabridged edition (New York: Union Square Kids, 2014).
2. Disney, Walt, *Walt Disney's Version of Pinocchio* (New York: Grosset and Dunlap, 1939).
3. 1 Corinthians 13:11.
4. Matthew 13:53–58; see also Mark 6:2–4.
5. Nickell, Joe, "Blood of Jesus," *Relics of the Christ* (Lexington: University Press of Kentucky, 2007), 169–170.
6. Roadside America Team, "5,000 relics in St. Anthony's Chapel," roadsideamerica.com; see also saintanthonyschapel.org.
7. Ibid.
8. Nickell, *Relics of the Christ,* 169–170.
9. Moyer, Ginny Kubitz, "Who Were Mary's Parents? What Do We Know About Them?," *Busted Halo: Faith Shared Joyfully,* 26 Jul. 2012, bustedhalo.com.
10. Doctrine and Covenants 130:22.
11. "Nicene Creed," *Christian Reformed Church,* crcna.org; "The Nicene Creed, also called the Nicaeno-Constantinopolitan Creed, is a statement of the orthodox faith of the early Christian church in opposition to certain heresies, especially Arianism."
12. *Catechism of the Catholic Church,* Second Edition, point 463, Lebreria Editrice Vaticana, Nov. 2019.
13. Ibid.
14. John 4:24.
15. "What the Early Church Believed: God Has No Body," *Catholic Answers,* catholic.com/tract/god-has-no-body, retrieved 12 Dec. 2019.
16. Doctrine and Covenants 130:22.
17. Doctrine and Covenants 76:22–24.
18. Doctrine and Covenants 77:2.
19. Moses 2:26.
20. Doctrine and Covenants 131:7–8.
21. Isaiah 55:8–9.
22. Einstein, A., Podolsky, B., and N. Rosen, *Can Quantum-Mechanical Description of Physical Reality Be Considered Complete?* (1935), Physical Review, 47: 777–780.
23. Schrödinger, Erwin, *Discussion of probability relations between separated systems,* Mathematical Proceedings of the Cambridge Philosophical Society (1935), 31:555–563.
24. Maldacena, Juan, "Black holes, wormholes and the secrets of quantum spacetime," *Scientific American* (Nov. 2016), 315:26–31.
25. Sakmann, Kaspar, and Mark Kasevich, "Single shot simulations of dynamic quantum many-body systems," *Nature Physics* (2016), 12:451-454.
26. Watson and Crick, *Nature* 171 (1953), 737–38.
27. Poirier, B., "Bohmian Mechanics without Pilot Waves," *Chem Phys* (2010), 370:4–14.
28. Davis, John, "Strange behavior of quantum particles may indicate the existence of other parallel universes," *phys.org,* 3 Jun. 2015.

29. Ibid.
30. Ibid.
31. Maldacena, Juan, "Black holes, wormholes and the secrets of quantum spacetime," *Scientific American*, Nov. 2016, 315:26–31.
32. Moses 3:1–5

CHAPTER 6

LAZARUS

The story of Lazarus is found only in John chapter 11, and is not mentioned in any of the other Gospels:

> Now a certain man was sick, named Lazarus, of Bethany, the town of Mary and her sister Martha. . . . Therefore his sisters sent unto him [Jesus], saying, Lord, behold, he whom thou lovest is sick. When Jesus heard that, he said, This sickness is not unto death, but for the glory of God, that the Son of God might be glorified thereby. . . . When he had heard therefore that he was sick, he abode two days still in the same place where he was. Then after that saith he to his disciples, Let us go into Judæa again . . ..These things said he: and after that he saith unto them, Our friend Lazarus sleepeth; but I go, that I may awake him out of sleep. Then said his disciples, Lord, if he sleep, he shall do well. . . . Then said Jesus unto them [his disciples] plainly, Lazarus is dead. . . . Then when Jesus came, he found that he had lain in the grave four days already. . . . Then said Martha unto Jesus, Lord, if thou hadst been here, my brother had not died. . . . Then when Mary was come where Jesus was, and saw him, she fell down at his feet, saying unto him, Lord, if thou hadst been here, my brother had not died. . . .

> Jesus therefore . . . cometh to the grave. It was a cave, and a stone lay upon it. Jesus said, Take ye away the stone. Martha, the sister of him that was dead, saith unto him, Lord, by this time he stinketh: for he hath been dead four days. . . .
>
> And . . . he [Jesus] cried with a loud voice, Lazarus, come forth. And he that was dead came forth, bound hand and foot with graveclothes: and his face was bound about with a napkin. Jesus saith unto them, Loose him, and let him go.[1]

This is the story of Lazarus that I grew up with: Lazarus became sick and then died. Then, after he had lain in the grave four days, Jesus came and raised him from the dead. However, the discussion between Jesus and His disciples concerning Lazarus's condition is very interesting. First, we read in verse 4 that Jesus said, "This sickness is not unto death, but for the glory of God, that the Son of God might be glorified thereby." Then he stated in verse 11, "Our friend Lazarus sleepeth; but I go, that I may awake him out of sleep." Then comes the exchange reported in verses 12–14: "Then said his disciples, Lord, if he sleep, he shall do well. Howbeit Jesus spake of his death: but they thought that he had spoken of taking of rest in sleep. Then said Jesus unto them plainly, Lazarus is dead."

So was Lazarus dead or was he just asleep, or perhaps both? How could he be both asleep and dead? One condition that matches these criteria is a coma, in which a person may appear dead while still alive—and in a deep sleep.

A coma is a deep state of unconsciousness during which a person cannot be awakened and does not respond to stimuli.[2] Coma patients may not exhibit any detectable blood pressure, may have no detectable pulse, and may exhibit no spontaneous respiration.[3] In other words, for all practical purposes, a person who is in a coma appears to be dead.

The term "coma" is from the Greek *koma*, meaning a deep sleep, and was used as early as 400 BC in the Hippocratic corpus (*Epidemica*). Galen used the term in the second century AD. Subsequently, however, it hardly appears again in the known literature until the middle of the 17th century.[4] Therefore, even though some Greek physicians were aware of the concept, it may not have been part of the general knowledge among the common Jewish population in the first century AD. Today, even in the presence of sophisticated medical monitoring equipment, it is not always easy to determine for certain if a person is alive or dead.

An example from almost exactly the same date as the Lazarus case illustrates the complexity of determining death in the first century AD. In AD 37, no less a person than the Roman Emperor Tiberius, age 78, fell into a coma resulting from an illness. The Roman historian, Tacitus, writing some ninety years later, stated, "On the 15th of March, his breath failing, he was believed to have expired." Presumably this was the conclusion of Charicles, a Greek physician serving in the Roman Empire, who was attending Tiberius.[5] As Tiberius was presumed dead, Caligula was coronated in his stead. The only way the Romans discovered that Tiberius wasn't dead was that he woke up and asked for something to eat. This slight inconvenience to Caligula's plans was handled promptly, as Caligula's chamberlain, Macro, was sent to suffocate Tiberius the same day.[6] If a Greek physician, who as a group, was considered the best in the world at the time, was not able to distinguish between coma and death in the Roman Emperor, it is highly unlikely that such a differentiation could have been ascertained by a group of ordinary Jews.

I believe that in the case of Lazarus, there were some simpler and some more complex concepts to be considered. For example, "Martha, the sister of him that was dead, saith unto him, Lord, by this time he stinketh: for he hath been dead four days."[7] Martha understood a simpler concept, that after four days a dead body would begin to stink, but she did not understand the more complex reason: that oxidation and bacterial activity are the causes of such decomposition. She also did not understand, nor did anyone else at the time, the more complex concept that there are various kinds of "dead," which concept even modern medicine still struggles to comprehend and codify. Discussion of these more complex concepts, in my opinion, in no way detracts from the miraculous nature of Lazarus being raised from the dead.

The story of Lazarus is often cited as a *type* of the resurrection and is one of the last prophecies given by Christ of His own resurrection. I find it extraordinary that Luke, a physician, who listed several miracles of healing not mentioned in the other gospels: such as fever,[8] infirmity,[9] dropsy,[10] the ten lepers,[11] and even two other cases of Christ raising people from the dead;[12] never mentioned the raising of Lazarus from the dead—considered by many modern Bible scholars to be the greatest of all His miracles. Recall that as important as this miracle must have been, and still is, we would not even know about it if it were not for the gospel of John. I find it especially intriguing and odd that Luke would discuss in some detail an interaction between Mary and Martha[13] but never even mentioned that they had a brother named Lazarus, probably, at least in our day, one of the most famous Christians who ever lived, and certainly one of the most interesting medical cases ever to occur.

I agree with the discussion of miracles in the Bible Dictionary, "Miracles should not be regarded as deviations from the ordinary course of nature . . . Some lower law was in each case superseded by the action of a higher."[14] Concerning Lazarus, Jesus made a very interesting comment to His disciples, "And I am glad for your sakes that I was not there, to the intent ye may believe . . ."[15]

In his footnote on p. 467 of *Jesus the Christ*, Elder James Talmage said concerning Lazarus's four days in the tomb,

> On the very probable assumption that the journey from Bethany in Judea to the place where Jesus was, in Perea, would require one day, Lazarus must have died on the day of the messenger's departure; for this day and the two days that elapsed before Jesus started toward Judea, and the day required for the return, would no more than cover the four days specified. It was and still is the custom in Palestine as in other oriental countries to bury on the day of death.
>
> It was the popular belief that on the fourth day after death the spirit had finally departed from the vicinity of the corpse, and that thereafter decomposition proceeded uninhibited. This may explain Martha's impulsive though gentle objection to having the tomb of her brother opened four days after his death (John 11:39). It is possible that the consent of the next of kin was required for the lawful opening of a grave. Both Martha and Mary were present,

> and in the presence of many witnesses assented to the opening of the tomb in which their brother lay.[16]

This background provided by Talmage is part of the enormous value of his classic work, and this information about Jewish tradition is valuable to the Lazarus story. As incorrect as this tradition may be, that belief is significant in light of Jesus's delay in arriving, purposely waiting until that traditional time had passed for the spirit to permanently leave the vicinity of the body.

So was Lazarus actually alive or dead at the time Jesus arrived? Of course he was dead—by all the criteria available to people of the time—and even by most criteria today. Martha said to Jesus, "By this time he stinketh: for he hath been dead four days."[17] And yet, when Lazarus came out of the grave, he apparently didn't stink.

Another condition that is associated with death is livor mortis, blood pooling by gravity in lower parts of the body. Blood continues to circulate as long as it is being pumped by the heart, even if the heart is only contracting very lightly and infrequently. However, when the heart stops beating completely, circulation of the blood stops, and gravity pulls the blood toward the lower, dependent regions of the body. For example, if a person is lying on his or her back when the heart stops beating, blood will pool in the back of the head, trunk, and limbs. Livor mortis, therefore, also called postmortem staining, is seen as a reddish-blue staining of those low-lying dependent regions of the body. In the early phases of livor mortis, patches of discoloration start appearing in the dependent regions within one to three hours of death. The patches increase in size and spread across dependent regions of the body within four to six hours and fully developed livor mortis, with full staining, can be seen within six to eight hours of death.[18]

In addition to blood pooling during livor mortis, it also breaks down. Red blood corpuscles break open and release hemoglobin into the surrounding tissues. Hemoglobin releases its bound oxygen, which causes oxidative damage to the tissues. Therefore, even if the heart were rebooted after livor mortis has set in, the blood is no longer functional.

The laws of nature obviously have not changed in two thousand years, and, as we believe, miracles do not suspend the laws of nature. Martha was correct that after a person had been dead four days, the body would already be decaying and would stink, and livor mortis would be apparent—even in the winter or early spring. We learn in John 10:22, "And it was at Jerusalem the feast of the dedication, and it was winter."

If the brain is deprived of oxygen for a matter of minutes, even in the cold, brain damage can occur. The 1986 case of two-year-old Michelle Funk was a remarkable exception. She had been submerged in icy water for over an hour without, apparently, suffering brain damage.[19] These data suggest that, even in very cold conditions, the brain can last only an hour or so without permanent damage. Other organs, such as the heart and kidneys, can be equally, permanently damaged following similar oxygen deprivation.

I believe in miracles, but I do not believe that they can defy the laws of nature. It is my opinion that miracles occur by compliance with "higher laws" of nature, which we do not, at present, fully understand. For example, two thousand years ago, if our ancestors became aware of a man-made satellite orbiting the earth, such an event would indeed have been a miracle, but today we understand laws not known then that allow us to launch satellites. Likewise, if a person had diabetes Type I two thousand years ago, it would have been a fairly rapid death sentence. Now we understand laws not known then that can prolong a diabetic's life for many years.

Therefore, it is my opinion that if Lazarus had actually been dead for the full four days that, even being raised from the dead, he would have experienced permanent brain and other organ damage. Today, we are quite familiar with cases of coma, where patients, by all measurements available, appear to be dead, and indeed are sometimes declared dead, but then revive. In the nineteenth century, relatives sat up with the deceased until they were buried in case they woke up. And when they were buried, some were placed in a "safety coffin" with a cable leading to a bell on the surface that they could ring if they weren't dead and woke up.

In 2012, a neighbor, Mr. Qingwang, found 95-year-old Liu Xiufeng of Guangxi Province, China, dead in her bed, about two weeks after Ms. Xiufeng had received a head injury from a fall. Mr. Qingwang shook her and called her name, with no response. In accordance with local Chinese custom, the "dead" woman was placed into a coffin and left in her house for six days so that friends and relatives could come by to pay their respects. A wooden lid was placed on the coffin between visits but was not nailed down. After the six days, and one day before the funeral, Mr. Qingwang returned to Ms. Xiufeng's home and found the coffin empty, with the lid removed, and the corpse missing. Mr. Qingwang was so terrified that he ran out of the house and recruited help from the neighbors. They found Ms. Xiufeng in her kitchen, sitting on a stool, cooking a meal. She explained that she had awoken very hungry after being asleep for a long time. She said that she had to push on the coffin lid for quite some time in order to get it open.[20]

In January 2014, 24-year-old Paul Mutora of Kenya, tried to take his own life by drinking insecticide. He awoke 24 hours later on a slab in the morgue at Naivasha District Hospital—and terrified the attendants by coming back to life. One month later, in February 2014, a 78-year-old man, Walter Williams from Mississippi, was declared dead by a hospice nurse. He awoke the next day in a body bag at the Porter & Sons Funeral Home in Lexington. Two weeks later, Mr. Williams died for good. On November 6th of the same year, a Polish woman named Janina Kolkiewicz, was declared dead at age 91 years. After being dead for eleven hours, she awoke in the hospital morgue, complaining of being cold and hungry.[21]

These and at least 34 additional similar cases are examples of what, since 1982 when the phenomenon first appeared by that name in the medical literature, have been called the Lazarus phenomenon or Lazarus syndrome, also known as autoresuscitation after cardiac arrest. Even in our modern medical age, a clinical declaration of death is not as definitive as is usually assumed. Two types of death are currently defined: clinical death, which is defined as the absence of a heartbeat, pulse, and respiration, and biological death, which is defined as the absence of detectable brain activity. Several known medical conditions—such as catalepsy, torpidity, or coma—can make it impossible to determine whether a person is actually dead or alive, even in the presence of our most sophisticated medical monitoring equipment.[22]

It may be possible that Jesus, along with everyone else, fully believed Lazarus to be dead. Indeed, even by today's standards, he may have been declared dead. I believe that God told Jesus to raise

Lazarus from the dead, but told Him to terry two days before doing so (Jesus said, "I can of mine own self do nothing . . . because I seek not mine own will, but the will of the Father which hath sent me."[23]). I believe that, of course, God knew exactly what He was doing and He knew the higher law that allowed Lazarus to appear quite dead while preserving the function of all vital organs. I also believe that, whereas Jesus did exactly as He was told by God, God may not have revealed to Jesus all of the laws behind His directions. Perhaps this is precisely why Jesus referred to Lazarus as being dead, but not totally dead—He knew He could raise Lazarus from the dead because He was commanded to do so by the Father, but He may not have known by what means the miracle was to be accomplished. Martha believed that, after four days, Lazarus's body would stink from the decay setting in, but the scriptures do not tell us that when he came out of the tomb, he *actually did stink*. Two thousand years ago, I don't believe anyone but God knew the full medical concept of comas—not even Jesus. I do not believe that Jesus had to understand the mechanisms of His miracles to perform them, He only needed to obey His Father.

Was this, then, just a trick? Not on Jesus's part, as He probably was not aware that Lazarus was not actually dead. Was this just a trick on God's part? We may have to wait and ask Him that question when we have a chance to meet Him. It is my opinion that God did not put Lazarus into a coma; that occurred as a natural outcome of his illness. But certainly God knew of the coma (even knowing that it was going to happen and when Lazarus would recover) and used this circumstance to show the power He had given to Jesus—the power over life and death. Jesus said of this opportunity, "This sickness is not unto death, but for the glory of God, that the Son of God might be glorified thereby."[24] When Jesus arrived at the tomb, He "lifted up his eyes, and said, Father, I thank thee that thou hast heard me. And I knew that thou hearest me always: but because of the people which stand by I said it, that they may believe that thou hast sent me."[25]

Why would God do such a thing—if such a thing was done? Why did God have Jesus perform any miracle? By His miracles, the people believed, but also by His miracles the priests and other Jewish leaders hated Jesus and ultimately murdered Him. It is clear that this particular miracle was a type of the resurrection of the Savior. Even after this miracle, Christ's disciples found it hard to believe that He had risen from the dead. Beyond that, for additional information, we'll have to ask God someday. I'm also anxious to ask Luke why he didn't discuss perhaps the most famous Biblical medical case of all time. Luke described Jesus's raising the man from the dead being carried out of the city[26] (perhaps the greatest miracle associated with that particular man being raised from the dead was that Jesus somehow sensed that he was not completely dead—why didn't Christ raise every dead person He encountered?) and His raising the ruler of the synagogue's daughter from the dead. He even stated of the girl, "Weep not; she is not dead, but sleepeth."[27] Matthew also recounted that miracle.[28] Yet Luke and Matthew omitted the rising of Lazarus, for what reason we do not know. Biblical scholars believe that John's gospel was the last of the four to be written, and that he often filled in gaps in the other narratives. This is probably why the raising of Lazarus is recorded in John, but it still remains unclear why that miracle was overlooked by the other three gospel authors.

By the way, it isn't an easy task to bring someone out of a coma. Jesus stood at the entrance to the cave and "cried with a loud voice, Lazarus, come forth."[29] In so doing, Jesus had to believe that God would do the rest—whatever that was. At that time, and even now in many cases, God alone knows how to retrieve someone from a coma.

Today, there is a precise legal definition of death, which includes no pupil reaction to light or temperature stimulation. There is no evidence of respiration or circulation (including absence of circulation as indicated by angiography). Signs also include absence of jaw and gag reflex and no response to pain stimulation. All of these signs must persist for at least 12 hours, with body temperature above 86 °F (30 °C; which eliminates the possibility of resuscitation following cold-water drowning) and a flat-line electroencephalogram (evaluation of brain wave activity). These signs also have to be in the absence of head injury or drugs that could mimic death-like symptoms.[30] In spite of these definitions, there still remains debate within the medical community as to how precisely to define death and exactly what tests are needed to confirm it.

Two thousand years ago almost none of those signs could have been ascertained. As a result, death was much simpler then, and far less precisely determined. Based on the simple criteria of death two thousand years ago, a person in a coma could very well be considered to be dead but have a "sickness . . . not unto death."[31]

---

1. John 11:1–44.
2. Weyhenmyeye, James A. and Eve A. Gallman, *Rapid Review Neuroscience* (St Louis, MO: Mosby Elsevier, 2007), 177–79.
3. Aslanidis, Theodoros, "Resuscitation Aspects," *TechOpen* (2017), 64.
4. Koehler, Peter J. and Eelco F.M. Wijdicks, "Historical study of coma: looking back through medical and neurological texts," *Brain* (2008), 131:877–889.
5. *The Annals of Tacitus*, Book VI:50 (Loeb Classical Library edition of Tacitus, 1937) 243, retrieved from penelope.uchicago.edu/Thayer/E/Roman/Texts/Tacitus/Annals/6B*.html, 21 Jun. 2020.
6. Seager, Robin, *Tiberius* (Hoboken, NJ: John Wiley & Sons, 2008).
7. John 11:39.
8. Luke 4:38–39.
9. Luke 13:11–17.
10. Luke 14:1–6.
11. Luke 17:12–19.
12. Luke 7:12–17; 8:49–53.
13. Luke 10:38–41.
14. "Miracles," *Bible Dictionary*, www.churchofjesuschrist.org/study/scriptures/bd/.
15. John 11:15.
16. Talmage, James E., *Jesus the Christ* (Salt Lake City, UT: Covenant Communications, 2006), 467.
17. John 11:39.
18. Shedge, Rutwik, Kewal Krishan, Varsha Warrier, and Tanuj Kanchan, "Postmortem Changes," *National Library of Medicine: National Center for Biotechnology Information* (Treasure Island, FL: StatPearls Publishing, 2020), ncbi.nlm.nih.gov/books/NBK539741, retrieved 20 Jun. 2020.
19. Venosa, Ali, "Breaking Point: How Long Can Someone Go Without Breathing?" *Medical Daily*, 9 Dec. 2015, medicaldaily.com.
20. Lusher, Adam, "True tales of people coming back to life during funerals and in mortuaries after being declared dead," *Independent*, 27 Oct. 2017, independent.co.uk/news/world/halloween-come-back-life-waking-dead-funerals-mortuaries-confirm-russia-egypt-a8023916.html; retrieved 30 November 2019.
21. Whiteman, Honor, "The Lazarus phenomenon: When the 'dead' come back to life," *Medical News Today*, 26 May 2017, medicalnewstoday.com/articles/317645.php#1, retrieved 29 November 2019.
22. Ibid.
23. John 5:30.
24. John11:20–22.
25. John 11:41–42.
26. Luke 7:12–17.
27. Luke 8:49–53.
28. Matthew 9:18–26.
29. John 11:43.
30. See medical-dictionary.thefreedictionary.com/death.
31. John 11:4.

CHAPTER 7

HOW LONG WAS JESUS DEAD?

During His ministry, Jesus healed a man "possessed with a devil" who was blind and dumb, "insomuch that the blind and dumb both spake and saw."[1] "But when the Pharisees heard it, they said, "This fellow doth not cast out devils, but by Beelzebub the prince of the devils. And Jesus knew their thoughts, and said unto them, Every kingdom divided against itself is brought to desolation; and every city or house divided against itself shall not stand."[2] The dialog continued,

> Then certain of the scribes and of the Pharisees answered, saying, Master, we would see a sign from thee. But he answered and said unto them, An evil and adulterous generation seeketh after a sign; and there shall no sign be given to it, but the sign of the prophet Jonas: For as Jonas was three days and three nights in the whale's belly; so shall the Son of man be three days and three nights in the heart of the earth.[3]

John's account of what appears to be the same conversation, or a nearly identical conversation after Christ had driven the money changers from the temple, added an additional twist,

> Then answered the Jews and said unto him, What sign shewest thou unto us, seeing that thou doest these things? Jesus answered and said unto them, Destroy this temple,

> and in three days I will raise it up. Then said the Jews, Forty and six years was this temple in building, and wilt thou rear it up in three days? But he spake of the temple of his body.[4]

This conversation concerning the temple became the major point of blasphemy for which Christ was tried and crucified:

> Now the chief priests, and elders, and all the council, sought false witness against Jesus, to put him to death; But found none: yea, though many false witnesses came, yet found they none. At the last came two false witnesses, And said, This fellow said, I am able to destroy the temple of God, and to build it in three days. And the high priest arose, and said unto him, Answerest thou nothing? what is it which these witness against thee? But Jesus held his peace. And the high priest answered and said unto him, I adjure thee by the living God, that thou tell us whether thou be the Christ, the Son of God. Jesus saith unto him, Thou hast said: nevertheless I say unto you, Hereafter shall ye see the Son of man sitting on the right hand of power, and coming in the clouds of heaven. Then the high priest rent his clothes, saying, He hath spoken blasphemy; what further need have we of witnesses? behold, now ye have heard his blasphemy. What think ye? They answered and said, He is guilty of death.[5]

Christ's statement about the temple apparently also became the main point made by the people who were mocking Him while He hung on the cross: "And they that passed by reviled him, wagging their heads, And saying, Thou that destroyest the temple, and buildest it in three days, save thyself. If thou be the Son of God, come down from the cross."[6]

Sometime after this conversation with the scribes and of the Pharisees, and before Christ went to Jerusalem for the last time, "From that time forth began Jesus to shew unto his disciples, how that he must go unto Jerusalem, and suffer many things of the elders and chief priests and scribes, and be killed, and be raised again the third day."[7] This prophecy is repeated in the next chapter of Matthew (chapter 17): "And while they abode in Galilee, Jesus said unto them, The Son of man shall be betrayed into the hands of men: And they shall kill him, and the third day he shall be raised again. And they were exceeding sorry."[8]

Christ also made a point of teaching His apostles privately about His pending death and resurrection:

> And Jesus going up to Jerusalem took the twelve disciples apart in the way, and said unto them, Behold, we go up to Jerusalem; and the Son of man shall be betrayed unto the chief priests and unto the scribes, and they shall condemn him to death, And shall deliver him to the Gentiles to mock, and to scourge, and to crucify him: and the third day he shall rise again.[9]

Luke said of this private conversation(s) between Christ and the apostles, "And they understood none of these things: and this saying was hid from them, neither knew they the things which were spoken."[10]

Concerning Christ's death on the cross, we are told in John chapter 19:

> When Jesus therefore had received the vinegar, he said, It is finished: and he bowed his head, and gave up the ghost. The Jews therefore, because it was the preparation, that the bodies should not remain upon the cross on the sabbath day, (for that sabbath day was an high day,) besought Pilate that their legs might be broken, and that they might be taken away. Then came the soldiers, and brake the legs of the first, and of the other which was crucified with him. But when they came to Jesus, and saw that he was dead already, they brake not his legs: But one of the soldiers with a spear pierced his side, and forthwith came there out blood and water. And he that saw it bare record, and his record is true: and he knoweth that he saith true, that ye might believe. For these things were done, that the scripture should be fulfilled, A bone of him

> shall not be broken. And again another scripture saith, They shall look on him whom they pierced.[11]

Mark tells us that Pilate was surprised that Christ was already, and so quickly, dead. He even called his centurion to confirm that Christ was actually dead.[12] It usually took three or four days for someone to die from crucifixion. Of course, even though centurions dealt with death on a regular basis, they were not physicians, and as was discussed in the previous chapter, not even physicians could distinguish between death and a coma. For all intents and purposes, it really didn't matter much, because whether on the battlefield or on a cross, if a comatose person was simply neglected, they would be dead soon enough. Furthermore, again, even in our modern era, we recognize that death is "often" preceded by coma.[13]

Stephen Huff has stated, "Though coma is a common clinical presentation to the emergency department (ED), the actual frequency of coma at ED presentation is difficult to determine."[14] Because only 0.03% of people die in such a way that their organs are useful for transplant, the strict clinical and biological criteria of death, described in the previous chapter for transplants, are not applied to all people who die.[15] Therefore, even in a modern emergency room, it is not easy to distinguish comatose from dead cases.

Furthermore, even in our modern hospital settings, a person may be dead but not remain dead. Christof Koch, chief scientist of the MindScope program at the Allen Institute for Brain Science, described two such conditions: "cardiac arrest, in which the heart stops beating (the patient is 'coding,' in hospital jargon). The patient has not died, because the heart can be jump-started via cardiopulmonary resuscitation [CPR]." Without CPR, however, when the heart stops beating the person is considered to be dead. Koch continued, "Modern death requires irreversible loss of brain function . . .his or her electroencephalogram, or EEG, becomes isoelectric—in other words, flat." But even this isoelectric, flatline state is reversible. "When the entire brain has shut down because of complete power loss, the mind is extinguished, along with consciousness. If and when oxygen and blood flow are restored, the brain boots up, and the narrative flow of experience resumes."[16]

Given the distance between Golgotha and Pilate's palace on the opposite side of Jerusalem, one or two hours are likely to have expired by the time the soldiers had obtained permission to remove Christ from the cross. After He had apparently "given up the ghost" (but how did John determine this?) Christ had hung on the cross, slumped over, completely unresponsive. The soldiers did not break His legs, as they did the two malefactors, to speed up their apparent deaths so they could be removed from the cross before sunset. However, one of the soldiers jabbed Christ in the side with his pilum and out poured a combination of blood and water. Such an action would not be uncommon under military conditions. On a battlefield of the time, soldiers very likely kicked, prodded, or jabbed the bodies of dead enemies to ascertain if any were still alive and responsive. Jabbing Christ in the side with a spear may likely have been for a similar reason. Such an action, however, could not determine if Christ was dead or comatose and not responsive.

A spear thrust to the side, into the abdominal cavity, may not necessarily be immediately fatal. I used to home teach an elderly gentleman who told me the story of his being severely wounded during the Korean War. He had a terrible abdominal injury to the extent that his intestines were hanging out. He slid under a building to hide from the enemy and spent the night holding in his bowels with his hand until he was rescued the next day.

We now know that dead people don't bleed fresh blood,[17] but, under conditions of internal hemorrhaging before death, there may be old, dark blood in the peritoneal cavity (the space within the abdomen) when opened after death. Over my forty-year career as an anatomist, I have seen dark blood mixed with fluid in the pleural cavity (around the lungs) and/or the peritoneal cavity many times. Whether Christ was dead or comatose would depend on the nature of the blood coming out of the wound in His side. Water, or clear fluid, may be a sign of edema and such fluid can empty from any body cavity of a cadaver.

Elder James E. Talmage proposed that such fluid came from Christ's pericardial cavity and indicated that He had died of a "broken heart."[18] However, fluid can also drain from the peritoneal cavity in the abdomen, especially if the body has been subjected to trauma, such as flogging and crucifixion. If a person dies of internal hemorrhage, which may not have occurred in Christ's case, unless He was also kicked in the abdomen during His flogging, then the fluid draining from the body cavity might be mixed with very dark blood. If the blood was lighter in color, however, such would indicate that the heart was still pumping aerated blood, however feebly, throughout the body. The nature of the blood exiting Christ's side wound was not distinguished in John's account.

Nonetheless, the composition of Christ's blood is critical to understand, because had it been quite dark, that sign would have indicated that His tissues were already beginning to decompose and putrefy, and even when revived, would not be functional at the cellular level (see the discussion below). At this point, therefore, I argue that Christ's body was not dead in the biological sense, but was cataleptic, torpid, or comatose. Of course, everyone attending the crucifixion, including the centurion, believed Him to be dead dead. If Christ had lapsed into catalepsis or coma on the cross, He likely would have remained in that condition while He was taken from the cross and carried to the garden tomb.

However private the earlier discussion might have been between Christ and His apostles concerning His death and resurrection, and as little as the apostles appeared to understand at that time, the chief priests and Pharisees were apparently well aware of Christ's prediction of His resurrection, and to which temple He was actually referring, for:

> Now the next day [after Christ's crucifixion], that followed the day of the preparation, the chief priests and Pharisees came together unto Pilate, Saying, Sir, we remember that that deceiver said, while he was yet alive, After three days I will rise again. Command therefore that the sepulchre be made sure until the third day, lest his disciples come by night, and steal him away, and say unto the people, He is risen from the dead: so the last error shall be worse than the first. Pilate said unto them, Ye have a watch: go your way, make it as sure as ye can. So they went, and made the sepulchre sure, sealing the stone, and setting a watch.[19]

The sequence of events that actually played out between Christ's apparent death on the cross and His resurrection the third day was as follows: "about the ninth hour [3 p.m.] . . . Jesus, when he had cried again with a loud voice, yielded up the ghost" (Matthew's account).[20] John's account adds this detail: Jesus "said, It is finished: and he bowed his head, and gave up the ghost."[21] Luke's account adds yet another detail: "And when Jesus had cried with a loud voice, he said, Father, into thy hands I commend my spirit: and having said thus, he gave up the ghost."[22]

There is not much information in the scriptures concerning what happened to Jesus's body for the next four hours. Then,

> When the even was come [probably around sundown, about 7 p.m.], there came a rich man of Arimathæa, named Joseph, who also himself was Jesus' disciple: He went to Pilate, and begged the body of Jesus. Then Pilate commanded the body to be delivered. And when Joseph had taken the body, he wrapped it in a clean linen cloth, And laid it in his own new tomb, which he had hewn out in the rock: and he rolled a great stone to the door of the sepulchre, and departed.[23]

So Christ's body apparently remained hanging on the cross from about 3 p.m. until sometime after 7 p.m. Luke's account adds that, "And the women also, which came with him [Jesus] from Galilee, followed after, and beheld the sepulchre, and how his body was laid. And they returned, and prepared spices and ointments; and rested the sabbath day [Saturday] according to the commandment."[24]

Luke's account then continues,

> Now upon the first day of the week, very early in the morning, they came unto the sepulchre, bringing the spices which they had prepared, and certain others with them. And they found the stone rolled away from the sepulchre. And they entered in, and found not the body of the Lord Jesus. And it came to pass, as they were much perplexed thereabout, behold, two men stood by them in shining garments: And as they were afraid, and bowed down their faces to the earth, they said unto them, Why seek ye the living among the dead? He is not here, but is

> risen: remember how he spake unto you when he was yet in Galilee, Saying, The Son of man must be delivered into the hands of sinful men, and be crucified, and the third day rise again.[25]

Matthew's account adds that "Mary Magdalene and the other Mary" came to the sepulcher, "in the end of the sabbath, as it began to dawn toward the first day of the week."[26] Matthew's account differs from that of Luke in stating that, rather than "two men" standing by them, the women beheld an "angel of the Lord . . .[whose] countenance was like lightning, and his raiment white as snow" sitting upon the stone, which he had rolled back from the sepulcher entrance.[27] The angel "said unto the women, Fear not ye: for I know that ye seek Jesus, which was crucified. He is not here: for he is risen, as he said. Come, see the place where the Lord lay."[28]

Mark's account of the angel differed yet more, "And entering into the sepulchre, they saw a young man sitting on the right side, clothed in a long white garment; and they were affrighted. And he saith unto them, Be not affrighted: Ye seek Jesus of Nazareth, which was crucified: he is risen; he is not here: behold the place where they laid him."[29]

John's account adds the detail that "it was yet dark" when Mary Magdalene came to the sepulcher.[30] If sunrise in Jerusalem was around 6:30 a.m. in early April, then Christ had been "dead" from around 3 p.m. on Friday until sometime before 6:30 a.m. Sunday—a maximum of 39 ½ hours. We do not know, however, how long before the women came to the sepulcher, Jesus had actually risen. Christ prophesied that He would die and then rise on the third day, which would have begun, according to Jewish tradition, at sunrise Sunday. He did not state, however, how long He would be dead. Therefore, an estimate of 40 hours should be about correct for the period of Christ's morbidity, if He was dead that entire time. He was in the sepulcher for somewhere around 35 hours.

Modern transplant protocol indicates that after the heart stops beating, vital organs become unusable for whole organ transplant very quickly. For example, hearts should be harvested for transplant within thirty minutes of death by exsanguination.[31] "But . . .tissues—such as bone, skin, heart valves and corneas—can be donated within the first 24 hours of death."[32]

Therefore, if a person is dead for an extended period of time—i.e. perhaps as much as 40 hours as in Jesus's case—permanent tissue and organ damage is almost certain upon revival. But resurrection is certainly much different from simple medical revival. We are promised that "For as in Adam all die, even so in Christ shall all be made alive."[33] Therefore, everyone born on earth will be resurrected because of Christ's resurrection. However, for the vast majority of humans who have ever lived, complete, or nearly complete deterioration of all tissues will have occurred before our resurrection.

There are two scriptural "accounts" of resurrected beings. The first is when Ezekiel, being carried "out in the spirit," was shown a valley full of dry bones and was commanded to prophesy that "the Lord God [will say] unto these bones; Behold, I will cause breath to enter into you, and ye shall live: And I will lay sinews upon you, and will bring up flesh upon you, and cover you with skin, and put breath in you, and ye shall live; and ye shall know that I am the Lord." And Ezekiel saw the bones come together, and "the sinews and the flesh came up upon them, and the skin covered them above." And the four winds, breathed "upon these slain, that they may live."[34] It is my opinion that Ezekiel saw metaphorically in vision what will happen at the resurrection. For most people, there will be no actual bones to come together because they will have been completely deteriorated. Therefore, the resurrection must be a de novo event, which will be discussed in detail in a later chapter.

The second account is that after Christ was resurrected, "the graves were opened; and many bodies of the saints which slept arose, And came out of the graves after his resurrection, and went into the holy city, and appeared unto many."[35] Whereas it is quite certain that many people in Jerusalem saw resurrected beings after Christ's resurrection, the concept that "graves were opened; and many bodies of the saints which slept arose," in my opinion is also metaphorical—as will be discussed later.

It is my opinion that Christ's resurrection was unique—orchestrated specifically to show His disciples that the resurrection was genuine. He was resurrected within 40 hours of His death, and it was apparently, literally His actual, intact mortal body that was resurrected, which will certainly not be the case for most people who have lived and died. For most people, our physical bodies will decay back into the earth from which they were made.[36] Except that after Christ's second coming, "In that day an infant shall not die until he is old; and his life shall be as the age of a tree; And when he dies he shall not sleep, that is to say in the earth, but shall be changed in the twinkling of an eye, and shall be caught up, and his rest shall be glorious."[37] In Christ's case, His tomb was empty, His physical body was gone, He had apparently walked out of the tomb with the same body that had been laid in the tomb.

In order for Christ's body to be resurrected intact, so that it could walk out of the tomb, it needed to be preserved in pristine condition for those 40 hours. The average temperatures in Jerusalem for early April, at the time of Christ's death, would have varied from a low of 40–55° F (an ideal refrigerator temperature is 40°F) to a high of 55–75° F. A cave tomb would have preserved the body at a much more constant, cool temperature. But even under those conditions, deterioration would have occurred over a forty-hour period.

In my opinion, the most likely scenario is that Christ was not actually dead for that entire 40-hour period. It is possible that He was not yet dead when placed into the tomb but was initially in a state of catalepsy, torpidity, or coma, which, as discussed in the previous chapter, may be characterized by a person being in a trance-like state, with complete immobility, no perceptible heart rate or respiration, and no apparent response to outside stimulation. These states may last from several minutes to several weeks or even months. Perhaps Lazarus was indeed a type of Jesus's resurrection, pointing not only toward the event but also the higher law applying to both events. Not even the medical experts of the time could have distinguished catalepsy from death.

In the case of Lazarus, we have no information as to whether his spirit remained in his body during his comatose state or whether it separated from his body for part or all of the four days he was considered to be dead. My opinion is that the latter was the case for at least part of that time. Historically and traditionally, it has been thought that the spirit actually provided the life of the body. However, there are no scriptural or scientific data to substantiate such a belief. This idea that the spirit is equivalent to life probably originates from the mistaken notion, which will be discussed in a later chapter, that breath and spirit are synonymous. Indeed, modern biochemistry and physiology suggest that life is a chemical process, which continues without any separate force, such as a vital spirit being present. Whereas some people might believe that this scientific evidence renders belief in a spirit archaic, it is my opinion that the only thing rendered archaic is the false belief that the spirit is equivalent to life, is equivalent to breath. I believe that the relationship between the body and the spirit is far more complex, far more arcane, and far more interesting than the simplistic relationship hitherto believed.

Despite the fact that we have no information about Lazarus's spirit during his four-day confinement, we do have such information about Christ's three-day entombment. Jesus taught, while yet alive that:

> Verily, verily, I say unto you, The hour is coming, and now is, when the dead shall hear the voice of the Son of God: and they that hear shall live. For as the Father hath life in himself; so hath he given to the Son to have life in himself; And hath given him authority to execute judgment also, because he is the Son of man. Marvel not at this: for the hour is coming, in the which all that are in the graves shall hear his voice, And shall come forth; they that have done good, unto the resurrection of life; and they that have done evil, unto the resurrection of damnation.[38]

We also read in 1 Peter chapter 3,

> For Christ also hath once suffered for sins, the just for the unjust, that he might bring us to God, being put to death in the flesh, but quickened by the Spirit: By which also he went and preached unto the spirits in prison; Which sometime were disobedient, when once the longsuffering of God waited in the days of Noah, while the ark was a preparing, wherein few, that is, eight souls were saved by water.[39]

Further, we read in 1 Peter 4: 6: "For for this cause was the gospel preached also to them that are dead, that they might be judged according to men in the flesh, but live according to God in the spirit."[40] Paul challenged the Corinthians, who were doubting a literal resurrection, "Else what shall they do which are baptized for the dead, if the dead rise not at all? why are they then baptized for the dead?"[41] Clearly the early saints understood that part of being "judged according to men in the flesh" included the saving ordinances, such as baptism, and that these ordinances could be performed by the living for the dead.

On 3 October 1918, in Salt Lake City, Utah, President Joseph F. Smith sat in his room, "pondering over the scriptures; And reflecting upon the great atoning sacrifice that was made by the Son of God, for the redemption of the world."[42] On that occasion, President Smith stated that he "opened the Bible and read the third and fourth chapters of the first epistle of Peter, and as I read I was greatly impressed, more than I had ever been before," especially with the verses quoted in the previous two paragraphs.[43]

> As I pondered over these things which are written, the eyes of my understanding were opened, and the Spirit of the Lord rested upon me, and I saw the hosts of the dead, both small and great. And there were gathered together in one place an innumerable company of the spirits of the just, who had been faithful in the testimony of Jesus while they lived in mortality; And who had offered sacrifice in the similitude of the great sacrifice of the Son of God, and had suffered tribulation in their Redeemer's name. All these had departed the mortal life, firm in the hope of a glorious resurrection, through the grace of God the Father and his Only Begotten Son, Jesus Christ. I beheld that they were filled with joy and gladness, and were rejoicing together because the day of their deliverance was at hand. They were assembled awaiting the advent of the Son of God into the spirit world, to declare their redemption from the bands of death. Their sleeping dust was to be restored unto its perfect frame, bone to his bone, and the sinews and the flesh upon them, the spirit and the body

> to be united never again to be divided, that they might receive a fulness of joy.
>
> While this vast multitude waited and conversed, rejoicing in the hour of their deliverance from the chains of death, the Son of God appeared, declaring liberty to the captives who had been faithful; And there he preached to them the everlasting gospel, the doctrine of the resurrection and the redemption of mankind from the fall, and from individual sins on conditions of repentance. But unto the wicked he did not go, and among the ungodly and the unrepentant who had defiled themselves while in the flesh, his voice was not raised; Neither did the rebellious who rejected the testimonies and the warnings of the ancient prophets behold his presence, nor look upon his face.[44]

President Smith went on the explain,

> But his [the Savior's] ministry among those who were dead was limited to the brief time intervening between the crucifixion and his resurrection; And I wondered at the words of Peter—wherein he said that the Son of God preached unto the spirits in prison, who sometime were disobedient, when once the long-suffering of God waited in the days of Noah—and how it was possible for him to preach to those spirits and perform the necessary labor among them in so short a time.
>
> And as I wondered, my eyes were opened, and my understanding quickened, and I perceived that the Lord went not in person among the wicked and the disobedient who had rejected the truth, to teach them; But behold, from among the righteous, he organized his forces and appointed messengers, clothed with power and authority, and commissioned them to go forth and carry the light of the gospel to them that were in darkness, even to all the spirits of men; and thus was the gospel preached to the dead.
>
> And the chosen messengers went forth to declare the acceptable day of the Lord and proclaim liberty to the captives who were bound, even unto all who would repent

> of their sins and receive the gospel. Thus was the gospel preached to those who had died in their sins, without a knowledge of the truth, or in transgression, having rejected the prophets. These were taught faith in God, repentance from sin, vicarious baptism for the remission of sins, the gift of the Holy Ghost by the laying on of hands, And all other principles of the gospel that were necessary for them to know in order to qualify themselves that they might be judged according to men in the flesh, but live according to God in the spirit. And so it was made known among the dead, both small and great, the unrighteous as well as the faithful, that redemption had been wrought through the sacrifice of the Son of God upon the cross.
>
> Thus was it made known that our Redeemer spent his time during his sojourn in the world of spirits, instructing and preparing the faithful spirits of the prophets who had testified of him in the flesh; That they might carry the message of redemption unto all the dead, unto whom he could not go personally, because of their rebellion and transgression, that they through the ministration of his servants might also hear his words.[45]

These scriptures make it very clear that for at least part, if not all the time that Christ's body was on the cross (around four hours after He had "given up the ghost") and/or laid in the tomb (some 35 hours), His spirit was preparing the work of redemption in the spirit world. His condition during at least the first four hours—before His body was placed into the tomb—would seem to imply that He was dead and that His spirit was not with His body. However, there is no scriptural or scientific evidence that the spirit cannot leave the body of a comatose person. Once His body was laid into the tomb and the entrance was covered with a stone, however, we know nothing of what happened to His body until the stone was removed some time before sunrise on Sunday. Furthermore, in some way during that entire 40 hours, His body was preserved in such a manner that it did not decompose. Perhaps His body was in a state of catalepsy for most of that time, and then it was resurrected in the twinkling of an eye.[46]

As difficult as it is to determine when a person is actually dead, it is far more difficult, if not impossible, to determine when a person's spirit may leave from or return to a dead, or even a comatose, body. Perhaps the most famous life after death, out-of-body experience, at least my favorite, is that of George G. Ritchie, Jr. In 1943, Ritchie, a twenty-year-old US Army private, stationed at Camp Barkeley, Texas, was awaiting transfer on December 18th to Virginia where, "On December 22 [he] . . .was going to start classes at the Medical College of Virginia, in [his] . . .home-town of Richmond, to become a doctor under the Army Specialized Training Program." He had completed his undergraduate pre-med training at the University of Richmond "at nineteen, doing the four-year course in two, as many were doing during the war," and had been accepted to medical school, but on December 11th he developed symptoms of pneumonia and was transferred to the isolation unit of the five-thousand-bed base barracks-hospital, where he died on December 21st. He had no detectable respiration, pulse, or blood pressure, and was declared dead. Nine minutes later the "ward boy" returned to the small room into which his body had been placed and noticed that his hand moved.[47]

During his nine-minute out-of-body experience, Ritchie found himself running through the air toward Richmond, and medical school. Finally, he stopped on the east bank of the Mississippi River—in front of a small, white, frame café—after wondering if he was going the right direction and deciding to stop and ask where he was. He floated down some fifty feet to the sidewalk, but a man he tried to ask acted like Ritchie wasn't even there. He realized that perhaps nobody could see him and decided that he must have left his "solidness," the "material, concrete" part of himself back at the base hospital and returned as quickly as he had left.

Several years later, he returned via automobile to the same location on the bank of the Mississippi.

> I knew I had never been there before, and yet I knew exactly how the shoreline would look around the next curve. How the streets would intersect. There! Just as I'd known they would! And all at once I knew for sure that straight ahead on that very street we would come in a few

> blocks to a white frame building with a red roof and the word 'Café' in neon letters over the door.[48]

To me, the most compelling part of this story is the fact that Ritchie was able to direct the car in which he was riding back to that very same café, which he had never seen in the flesh, but which he had only visited in the spirit. This story is almost unique in providing solid evidence for an experience that had occurred while the person was out of his body.

Christof Koch, who cited Raymond Moody as the person who coined the term "near-death experience," stated, "Unless there is extraordinary, compelling, objective evidence to the contrary, I see no reason to abandon this assumption . . . that all our thoughts, memories, percepts and experiences are an ineluctable consequence of the natural causal powers of our brain rather than of any supernatural ones."[49] Koch, however, failed to mention the "extraordinary, compelling, objective" story of George Ritchie, "a respected physician" who "profoundly impressed" Raymond Moody as "one of the three or four most fantastic and well-documented 'dying' experiences known to me."[50] Indeed, Moody dedicated his own book, *Life After Life*, to George Ritchie.[51]

Moody posited, "Was George Ritchie . . . really dead? . . . In the clinical sense . . . the whole matter of the final criteria for diagnosing death is very much up in the air just now, very much unsettled among the medical profession itself." To my knowledge, the veracity of Ritchie's account has never been impugned—rather it has been mostly, if not entirely, simply ignored, and the extraordinary nature of the account has been neglected, let alone the compelling and objective nature of the experience. Moody also observed, "Admittedly, if one defines 'death'—as seems eminently reasonable—as that state of the body from which restoration of function is impossible, then none of these people [Ritchie and others with similar stories] were dead."[52]

If Moody's assessment is correct, then the spirit of a cataleptic, torpid, or comatose person can leave the body and travel to distant sites before returning—and, at least in Ritchie's case, remember details of the trip. What makes Ritchie's experience so extraordinary is that his spirit left the immediate environs of his body. In all other near-death or out-of-body experiences of which I am aware the spirit remains near the body so that it is very difficult to distinguish spirit sensations from bodily sensations, or even memory bias.

Apparently, around ten percent of people claim to have had some sort of out-of-body experience (OBE). Spontaneous OBEs are most often reported by people as they are falling asleep or awakening, and appear to be exacerbated by stressful conditions that prevent restful sleep, such as noise, mental tension, or illness. OBEs have also been reported by people who are awake and have undergone extreme mental or physical exertion, or who are in possible life-threatening situations. One 36-year-old police officer reported that during her first night on duty, "When I and three other officers stopped the vehicle and started getting [to] the suspect [. . .] I was afraid. I promptly went out of my body and up into the air maybe 20 feet above the scene. I remained there, extremely calm, while I watched the entire procedure—including watching myself do exactly what I had been trained to do."[53]

Christophe Lopez and Maya Elzière stated that, "Out-of-body experiences (OBEs) are states during which people experience their centre of awareness as located outside of their physical body, along with the sensation of seeing the environment from an elevated viewpoint." After examining 210 patients with OBEs and dizziness, they concluded, "Altogether, our data indicate that OBE in patients with dizziness may arise from a combination of perceptual incoherence evoked by the vestibular dysfunction with psychological factors (depersonalization-derealization, depression and anxiety) and neurological factors (migraine)."[54] Although Lopez and Elzière's findings are very interesting concerning localization of many OBEs, they do not explain all ODEs or near-death experiences (NDEs). Certainly the vast majority of ODEs and even NDEs can be explained by our own neurological functions; however, there remains a tiny fraction, of which Ritchie is to my knowledge the most compelling, that cannot be so explained.

All this said, I will now return to Christ's time in the tomb. He was apparently entombed for some 35 hours, during which time His spirit left His body and ministered to spirits in prison,[55] or more specifically, organized a mission to those prisoners.[56] During most of those 35 hours He may not have been dead, but may have been in a state of catalepsy, torpidity, or coma. Sometime during those 35 hours, however, it was apparently necessary for Him to actually die.[57] But the time between His actual death and resurrection may have been extremely short, perhaps even as short as the twinkling of an eye,[58] so that His cellular structure did not have time to break down between His death and resurrection. This conclusion in no way diminishes the reality of Christ's death and resurrection or the impact His Atonement has on our own resurrections.

---

1. Matthew 12:22.
2. Matthew 12:24–25.
3. Matthew 12:38–40.
4. John 2:18–21.
5. Matthew 26:59–66; see also Mark 14:55–58.
6. Matthew 27:39–40; see also Mark 15:29–30.
7. Matthew 16:21.
8. Matthew 17:22–23.
9. Matthew 20:17–19; see also Mark 9:30–31; 10:32–34; Luke 9:18–22; 18:31–34.
10. Luke 18:34.
11. John 19:30–37.
12. Mark 15:44.
13. "Signs of Approaching Death," *Hospice Foundation of America*, hospicefoundation.org/Hospice-Care/Signs-of-Approaching-Death; retrieved 27 Jun. 2020.
14. Huff, J. Stephen, "Coma," *StatPearls* (2020), retrieved 27 Jun. 2020.
15. "Organ Donation Statistics," *Health Resources & Services Administration,* organdonor.gov/statistics-stories/statistics.html, retrieved 28 Jun. 2020.
16. Koch, Christof, "Tale of the Dying Brain," *Scientific American* (July 2020), 74.
17. Engelhaupt, Erika, "How Talking Corpses Were Once Used to Solve Murders," *National Geographic*, October 9, 2017, nationalgeographic.com/science/article/how-talkingcorpses-solve-murders-cruentation-ordeal-science.
18. Talmage, James E., *Jesus the Christ* (Salt Lake City, Utah: The Church of Jesus Christ of Latter-day Saints, 2006), chapter 35, note 8.
19. Matthew 27:62–66.
20. Matthew 27:46, 50.
21. John 19:30.
22. Luke 23:46.
23. Matthew 27:57–60; see also Mark 15:42–47; Luke 23:50–53; John 19:38–42.
24. Luke 23:55–56.
25. Luke 24:1–7.
26. Matthew 28:1.
27. Matthew 28:2–3.
28. Matthew 28:5–6.
29. Mark 16:5–6.
30. John 20:1.
31. Gundry, SR, JA de Begona, M. Kawauchi, and LL Bailey, "Successful transplantation of hearts harvested 30 minutes after death from exsanguination," *Ann Thorac Surg* (1992), 53:772–4.
32. Machado, C, A definition of human death should not be related to organ transplants, Journal of Medical Ethics, 29, 2003, jme.bmj.com/content/29/3/201.
33. 1 Corinthians 15:22.
34. Ezekiel 37:1–14.

35. Matthew 27:52–53.
36. Genesis 3:19.
37. Doctrine and Covenants 101:30–31.
38. John 5:25–29.
39. 1 Peter 3:18–20.
40. 1 Peter 4:6.
41. 1 Corinthians 15:29.
42. Doctrine and Covenants 138:1–2.
43. Doctrine and Covenants 138:6–10.
44. Doctrine and Covenants 138:11–21.
45. Doctrine and Covenants 138:27–37.
46. Doctrine and Covenants 101:30–31.
47. Ritchie, George G., and Sherrill, Elizabeth, *Return from Tomorrow* (Old Tappan, NJ: Revell, 1978), 18–79.
48. Ibid, 97–98.
49. Koch, Christof, "Tale of the Dying Brain," *Scientific American* (July 2020), 73.
50. Moody, Raymond, Foreword to *Return from Tomorrow*, by George G. Ritchie and Elizabeth Sherrill (Old Tappan, NJ: Revell, 1978).
51. Moody, Raymond A., *Life After Life* (Bantam Books, 1976).
52. Moody, Raymond, Foreword to *Return from Tomorrow*, by George G. Ritchie and Elizabeth Sherrill (Old Tappan, NJ: Revell, 1978).
53. Newman, Tim, "Out-of-body experiences: Neuroscience or the paranormal?" *Medical News Today*, 19 Jul. 2017, medicalnewstoday.com/articles/318464.php#1; retrieved 4 Dec. 2019.
54. Lopez, Christophe, and Maya Elzière, "Out-of-body Experience in Vestibular Disorders - A Prospective Study of 210 Patients With Dizziness," *Cortex* (2018), 104:193–206.
55. 1 Peter 3:18–20
56. Doctrine and Covenants 138:27–37.
57. 1 Thessalonians 4:14.
58. Doctrine and Covenants 101:30–31.

CHAPTER 8

VISIT TO THE SPIRIT WORLD

We now know because of modern organ transplant work that a person may be dead without the tissues being too far deteriorated to transplant. Likewise with Christ. He must have been in such a vegetative state that His body was "dead" as to muscular movement, or even detectable respiration or even heartbeat, but His tissues were in such a state that Sunday morning they could be reanimated, and He could walk out of the tomb.

During the time that Christ's body was lying in the tomb, His spirit visited the spirit world. We are told, by way of a vision given to President Joseph F. Smith in Salt Lake City, Utah, on October 3, 1918, when he was sitting in his room "pondering over the scriptures,"

> For for this cause was the gospel preached also to them that are dead, that they might be judged according to men in the flesh, but live according to God in the spirit.[1]
>
> For Christ also hath once suffered for sins, the just for the unjust, that he might bring us to God, being put to death in the flesh, but quickened by the Spirit: By which also he went and preached unto the spirits in prison; Which sometime were disobedient, when once the longsuffering of God waited in the days of Noah, while the ark was a preparing, wherein few, that is, eight souls were saved by water.[2]

President Smith stated,

> As I pondered over these things which are written, the eyes of my understanding were opened, and the Spirit of the Lord rested upon me, and I saw the hosts of the dead, both small and great . . . While this vast multitude waited and conversed, rejoicing in the hour of their deliverance from the chains of death, the Son of God appeared, declaring liberty to the captives who had been faithful; And there he preached to them the everlasting gospel, the doctrine of the resurrection and the redemption of mankind from the fall, and from individual sins on conditions of repentance. But unto the wicked he did not go, and among the ungodly and the unrepentant who had defiled themselves while in the flesh, his voice was not raised; Neither did the rebellious who rejected the testimonies and the warnings of the ancient prophets behold his presence, nor look upon his face . . . But his ministry among those who were dead was limited to the brief time intervening between the crucifixion and his resurrection;
>
> And I wondered at the words of Peter—wherein he said that the Son of God preached unto the spirits in prison, who sometime were disobedient, when once the long-suffering of God waited in the days of Noah—and how it was possible for him to preach to those spirits and perform the necessary labor among them in so short a time.
>
> And as I wondered, my eyes were opened, and my understanding quickened, and I perceived that the Lord went not in person among the wicked and the disobedient who had rejected the truth, to teach them; But behold, from among the righteous, he organized his forces and appointed messengers, clothed with power and authority, and commissioned them to go forth and carry the light of the gospel to them that were in darkness, even to all the spirits of men; and thus was the gospel preached to the dead. And the chosen messengers went forth to declare the acceptable day of the Lord and proclaim liberty to the

> captives who were bound, even unto all who would repent of their sins and receive the gospel.[3]

Section 138 was not added to the Doctrine and Covenants until the 1981 edition.[4] As a result, I didn't get to learn this marvelous section as a student in seminary or even as a BYU student. I didn't get to teach this marvelous section as a young missionary. All I got to do was teach 1 Peter 3:18–20 and 4:6 without the powerful prophetic interpretation we can now add to those passages. What a wonderful time we live in when the doors of the heavenly library are being flung open and all we have to do is walk in and start pulling books off the shelves! Thank you President Smith for pondering the scriptures!

The other great revelation we receive from this marvelous section is that the spirit is not necessary to keep the body alive. This is a question that I have pondered for many years and have discussed and debated with many friends and fellow students. While Christ's body lie in a vegetative, comatose state in the tomb awaiting the resurrection, with His tissues in a tissue-donor, preserved state and His brain perhaps even flat-lined in a clinically dead condition, His spirit was in the spirit world preparing the righteous spirits to preach the gospel in the spirit prison.

Therefore, it may be concluded that the spirit is not necessary to maintain life, at least at a vegetative state. Life is a physiological condition, not a condition where the spirit somehow infuses some magical quality into the body that is not otherwise there.

---

1. 1 Peter 4:6.
2. 1 Peter 3:18–20.
3. Doctrine and Covenants 138:11, 18–21, 27–31.
4. Doctrine and Covenants, 1981 edition title page.

CHAPTER 9

THAT FIRST EASTER MORNING

"Now upon the first day of the week, very early in the morning, they came unto the sepulchre, bringing the spices which they had prepared, and certain others with them. And they found the stone rolled away from the sepulchre. And they entered in, and found not the body of the Lord Jesus. And it came to pass, as they were much perplexed thereabout, behold, two men stood by them in shining garments: And as they were afraid, and bowed down their faces to the earth, they said unto them, Why seek ye the living among the dead? He is not here, but is risen:

"Remember how he spake unto you when he was yet in Galilee, Saying, The Son of man must be delivered into the hands of sinful men, and be crucified, and the third day rise again. And they remembered his words, And returned from the sepulchre, and told all these things unto the eleven, and to all the rest. It was Mary Magdalene, and Joanna, and Mary the mother of James, and other women that were with them, which told these things unto the apostles. And their words seemed to them as idle tales, and they believed them not. Then arose Peter, and ran unto the sepulchre; and stooping down, he beheld the linen clothes laid by themselves, and departed, wondering in himself at that which was come to pass."[1]

"So they ran both together: and the other disciple [whom Jesus loved] did outrun Peter, and came first to the sepulchre. And he stooping down, and looking in, saw the linen clothes lying; yet went he not in. Then cometh Simon Peter following him, and went into the sepulchre, and seeth the linen clothes lie, And the napkin, that was about his head, not lying with the linen clothes, but wrapped together in a place by itself. Then went in also that other disciple, which came first to the sepulchre, and he saw, and believed. For as yet they knew not the scripture, that he must rise again from the dead. Then the disciples went away again unto their own home.

"But Mary stood without at the sepulchre weeping: and as she wept, she stooped down, and looked into the sepulchre, And seeth two angels in white sitting, the one at the head, and the other at the feet, where the body of Jesus had lain. And they say unto her, Woman, why weepest thou? She saith unto them, Because they have taken away my Lord, and I know not where they have laid him. And when she had thus said, she turned herself back, and saw Jesus standing, and knew not that it was Jesus. Jesus saith unto her, Woman, why weepest thou? whom seekest thou? She, supposing him to be the gardener, saith unto him, Sir, if thou have borne him hence, tell me where thou hast laid him, and I will take him away. Jesus saith unto her, Mary. She turned herself, and saith unto him, Rabboni; which is to say, Master. Jesus saith unto her, Touch me not; for I am not yet ascended to my Father: but go to my brethren, and say unto them, I ascend unto my Father, and your Father; and to my God, and your God. Mary Magdalene came and told the disciples that she had seen the Lord, and that he had spoken these things unto her."[2]

1. Luke 24:1–12.
2. John 20:4–18.

CHAPTER 10

THAT FIRST EASTER NIGHT

The two disciples with whom the resurrected Jesus walked to Emmaus and sat at meat, on the afternoon of His resurrection, "rose up the same hour, and returned to Jerusalem, and found the eleven gathered together, and them that were with them"[1] "at evening, being the first day of the week, when the doors were shut where the disciples were assembled for fear of the Jews."[2] "Saying, The Lord is risen indeed."[3]

> And as they thus spake, Jesus himself stood in the midst of them, and saith unto them, Peace be unto you. But they were terrified and affrighted, and supposed that they had seen a spirit. And he said unto them, Why are ye troubled? And why do thoughts arise in your hearts? Behold my hands and my feet, that it is I myself: handle me, and see; for a spirit hath not flesh and bones, as ye see me have.[4]

Matthew did not cover this event in his gospel. Rather, as the apostle most concerned with the Jews and the fulfillment of prophecy, he was concerned about "the watch" taking a bribe to declare, "His disciples came by night, and stole him away while we slept," adding that, "and this saying is commonly reported among the Jews until this day."[5]

Mark was apparently only a teenager at the time of this momentous event, even though he may have been among "them that were with them."[6] When he was a bit older, he first traveled with Paul and then with Peter, acting as the latter's scribe and interpreter. So Mark's very short account of the event was probably actually Peter's account—who obviously was an eye witness.[7] Peter/Mark stated, "After that [Christ's initial appearances on the morning of the resurrection] he appeared in another form unto two of them, as they walked, and went into the country. And they went and told it unto the residue: neither believed they them. Afterward he appeared unto the eleven as they sat at meat, and upbraided them with their unbelief and hardness of heart, because they believed not them which had seen him after he was risen."[8]

The physician, Luke, never met the Savior and did not know Him until he was taught the gospel by Paul. He then left his medical practice and became Paul's traveling companion. During his travels, Luke had the opportunity to discuss the Savior's ministry with the apostles and other disciples. From these numerous interviews, he compiled his gospel—and then the book of Acts—probably much of that book from his own observations.[9] Luke's gospel, much of it based on Mark's accounts, is the longest of the four testaments and, together with the Acts, constitute 27.5% of the New Testament.[10]

John's gospel was probably written last, after he had apparently read the other author's accounts. As a result, rather than telling his own story de novo, he often filled in the gaps or corrected the stories told by the others. Thus, in his account, John confirmed that Christ's appearance occurred "the same day at evening, being the first day of the week." He then added the detail, "the doors were shut where the disciples were assembled for fear of the Jews."[11] John then corrected Mark and Luke's accounts that there were eleven apostles present. John stated, "But Thomas, one of the twelve, called Didymus, was not with them when Jesus came."[12] With Judas Iscariot being absent from the time of the Last Supper, that left only ten apostles in the closed room when the Savior first appeared to them.

In order to understand Christ's resurrected body, we may ponder Luke's accounts of Christ's appearances to His disciples following His resurrection. He first appeared to two disciples as they journeyed to Emmaus, we read that after they reached Emmaus: "And it came to pass, as he sat at meat with them, he took bread, and blessed it, and brake, and gave to them. And their eyes were opened, and they knew him; and he vanished out of their sight."[13]

While Christ "sat at meat" with His two disciples at Emmaus, did He eat the "meat" or did He just watch them eat? We are not told for certain, but we can logically assume that as He "sat at meat," He ate with the disciples. A later encounter that same day, however, leaves no question about Christ's ability to consume food. On that occasion, Christ specifically *demonstrated* that He *could* eat food. After Christ appeared to the apostles, "he said unto them, Have ye here any meat? And they gave him a piece of a broiled fish, and of an honeycomb. And he took it, and did eat before them."[14]

It appears that Christ ate the fish and honeycomb specifically to prove to the apostles that he *could* eat—he ate "before them"—as in a demonstration. Was Christ just performing some sort of "trick" to "prove" He could eat—to what purpose? It doesn't seem reasonable that Christ would just swallow food to prove that He could—without His intending for *us* to ponder the implications of that event. I believe He consumed food to teach us important, eternal truths about resurrected beings—with huge implications. To me, Christ's purposeful gastrological demonstration provides critical data to our understanding the resurrection. Those data, apparently, tell us that the resurrected Savior's digestive tract was intact and functional. The implications of that information could not have been fully understood by any of His disciples or their contemporaries. However, it is very interesting that Luke, the physician, was the only gospel author to include this detail of Christ's first post-resurrection meeting with the apostles. Nor could the implications have been fully understood by anyone living more than a hundred years or so ago.

The Savior told His disciples, "I can of mine own self do nothing . . .I seek not mine own will, but the will of the Father which hath sent me."[15] Therefore, it appears that God *told* Jesus to demonstrate to the apostles that He could eat. It, therefore, appears that it is significant to God to let us know that the risen Christ could eat food. Christ told us that by seeing Him we are seeing God. Therefore, His gastrological demonstration must teach us that God, as an immortal, resurrected being with a body of flesh and bones, can consume food. It is obviously important to God that we know this truth about Him, as He commanded His Son, after His resurrection, to eat fish and honeycomb before the disciples—and that this event was recorded in the scriptures.

Furthermore, we have been told that the resurrected Savior can still partake of food and drink—at least that will be the case at the time of His Second Coming. He has told us:

> Behold, this is wisdom in me; wherefore, marvel not, for the hour cometh that I will drink of the fruit of the vine with you on the earth, and with Moroni, whom I have sent unto you to reveal the Book of Mormon, containing the fulness of my everlasting gospel, to whom I have committed the keys of the record of the stick of Ephraim.[16]

Of course, it is entirely possible that consuming and processing food by a resurrected, immortal body is completely different from the way it is consumed and processed by mortals. At least three issues, however, argue against that proposition. First, the resurrected Christ apparently had the same body configuration as when He was mortal—including at least lips, teeth, and tongue. He apparently produced speech in the same manner He had done previously. His closest disciples could not distinguish His resurrected body from a mortal body—even though, in several cases, they didn't quite recognize Him as the Jesus they had known. The disciples on the road to Emmaus seem to have thought Him to be a stranger, whereas, Mary thought He was a gardener. Maybe He appeared to be a different age, very likely with white hair rather than the dark hair they knew, or perhaps there was some other characteristic, but there seems no doubt that he looked completely human. His apostles in the closed room thought they had seen a spirit but He invited them to handle Him. Second, there is no evidence that Christ left any of His earthly digestive system stashed in the tomb, or anywhere else, in exchange for some other, immortal digestive system. When Christ walked out of the tomb, He apparently left with all of His systems intact and complete. There were apparently no organs left behind in the tomb. Third, formal logic and the scientific method teach us the principal of parsimony, which states that, without sufficient evidence to the contrary, the simplest explanation is most likely the correct explanation.

With these ideas in mind, let us assume that Christ's digestive tract was much the same after the resurrection as it was before, and then discuss what we now know about digestion. The data from the resurrected Christ's gastrological demonstration strongly suggest that resurrected beings have digestive systems where food is pulverized—by the teeth—mixed with digestive enzymes in the stomach and intestine, and where individual nutrient molecules are absorbed through the intestinal cells lining the alimentary canal. In mortals, those nutrients then pass into the intestinal blood supply and are disbursed by the pumping heart throughout the body where they are broken down to provide energy for cellular metabolism. Hemoglobin in the blood also carries oxygen from the lungs to the tissues, where metabolism takes place. None of this information was known by any human before the mid-nineteenth century. Before then, breathing, digestion, and blood functions were mysteries. The possibility certainly exists that the liquid transport medium in mortals, i.e. blood, may be replaced by some other liquid in resurrected beings. At present, we simply have too little information to propose such an alternative, and parsimony tells us, at the present time at least, to continue using the story of blood. However, the issue of blood will be discussed somewhat differently in later chapters.

Paul said to the Corinthians, "Now this I say, brethren, that flesh and blood cannot inherit the kingdom of God; neither doth corruption inherit incorruption."[17] Many people seem to take this phrase literally, believing that in heaven we will have bodies of flesh and bone but not flesh and blood. It is much more likely, however, that Paul was speaking metaphorically—describing the human condition. He said to the Galatians, "To reveal his Son in me, that I might preach him among the heathen; immediately I conferred not with flesh and blood: Neither went I up to Jerusalem to them which were apostles before me; but I went into Arabia, and returned again unto Damascus."[18] And to the Ephesians he said, "For we wrestle not against flesh and blood, but against principalities, against powers, against the rulers of the darkness of this world, against spiritual wickedness in high places."[19] In these last two scriptures, Paul seems to be using the term "flesh and blood" to refer to people in general.

Furthermore, if neither Paul, nor anyone else of his era, had any idea what blood actually did, why would they be so specific about there being no blood in heaven? Ancient people believed for thousands of years that blood was the corrupting principle in the body, but did not know why. They reasoned that if no corruption could enter heaven, then that must include blood. They also had no idea what the heart actually did—they believed it was the mind—it was the source of love and devotion and courage. They had no idea it was actually a pump that propelled blood throughout the body. Therefore, if there is no blood in heaven, then there would be no need for hearts there either. Do resurrected beings have no hearts? People seem to find it easier to believe there is no blood in heaven than that there are no hearts in heaven. Of course, if blood is replaced by some other fluid, which is "immortal" but has all the same functions as blood, then the resurrected, immortal heart may pump that immortal fluid. In any event, it seems likely that the resurrected heart will pump *something*. We simply haven't sufficient information to even hazard an intelligent guess at this time as to what that something might be—if not blood.

Glycolysis, also known as the Embden–Meyerhof pathway, which explains how humans break down carbon compounds from food to produce the energy necessary for life, was not fully worked out until the 1920s and 1930s in Germany by Gustav Embden, Otto Meyerhof, and others—the culmination of over one hundred years of research by several people.[20] Still, many people today have never even heard of glycolysis or Embden-Meyerhof. Those of us who have studied and written about this critical pathway know that the last breakdown products of glycolysis feed into the citric acid cycle, which, in turn, feeds into the electron transport chain. The last step in the electron transport chain, which transfers the energy stored in hydrogen bonds (electrons) to produce ATP (adenosine triphosphate, the energy currency of the body) is the transfer of an electron to oxygen.[21] Without oxygen as the terminal receptor in this long chain of events, the whole system comes to a screeching halt, not enough ATP is produced to sustain life, and the person dies within a matter of about six minutes.

Whereas a small portion of oxygen is dissolved in the plasma, most of the oxygen transported to the tissues (98.5%) is attached to hemoglobin molecules inside red blood corpuscles—it's the iron inside the hemoglobin molecule, bound to oxygen, that gives blood its red color. The connection between hemoglobin and oxygen was first proposed by the French physiologist Claude Bernard around 1870.[22] Just as critical as the delivery of oxygen to tissues, is the removal of CO_2, the waste product of glycolysis, from the tissues. If CO_2 accumulates in cells, glycolysis slows down or stops completely and death follows. Veins carry CO_2, dissolved in the blood, back to the lungs where it is exhaled and a new breath of oxygen-containing air is inhaled. Pulmonary veins carry this oxygenated blood to the heart, and arteries then carry the fresh supply of oxygen-containing blood to the tissues.

The problem is that oxygen is a double-edged sword. On the one hand, our very lives depend upon it, but on the other hand, it is one of the most dangerous elements on earth—or in the air. Oxidation is named for the processes involving oxygen—the rusting of metal, fruit turning dark, the aging process, and general deterioration throughout the world are often the result of oxidation. It is critical within our bodies that oxygen is kept away from most tissues. That is why it is held captive within hemoglobin molecules, inside red blood corpuscles, until it can be transferred to the mitochondria inside tissue cells where it is employed as the terminal receptor in the electron transport chain. If oxygen leaks out of the blood, such as occurs in a cerebral hemorrhage, oxygen in the blood will destroy the neurons with which it comes in contact. This double function of oxygen, life and death, is probably the greatest irony of mortality.

One way to combat oxidation is by means of antioxidants. We are constantly seeking, in our modern world, the perfect antioxidants to help combat disease and put off the aging process. Maybe, from an eternal perspective, antioxidants are the secret to immortality. Perhaps that was the function of the tree of life in the Garden of Eden. We are also told that there will be trees of life in the paradise of God.[23] Perhaps those trees of life will be the secret of our future immortality. But dependence on some outside source, such as the tree of life, for our immortality would appear to make that immortality conditional—yet as we contemplate immortality, such a condition seems counterintuitive.

Perhaps another solution to accomplishing immortality would be to get rid of our dependence on oxygen altogether. "Lay not up for yourselves treasures upon earth, where moth and rust doth corrupt . . . But lay up for yourselves treasures in heaven, where neither moth nor rust doth corrupt."[24] Possibly, the main difference between a mortal and an immortal being is that the oxygen-containing blood is replaced by some "spiritual" fluid in our veins and arteries that carry some other terminal receptor molecule for the electron transport chain. Or, maybe, the entire Embden–Meyerhof pathway—citric acid cycle—electron transport chain system will be replaced by some other enzymatic pathway in resurrected beings. We cannot, at present, propose what the elemental basis of such fluid might be. Oxygen occupies a unique position on the periodic table of the elements, and there is no place, that we know of at present, for any other element to accomplish the task performed by oxygen. Furthermore, at present, parsimony argues that it is far more likely that the mortal and immortal systems are more the same than they are different. If God has a heart, which I believe He has, then He has blood or some other fluid pumped by that heart throughout His body.

In our modern society, researchers are already looking for other fluids that can either supplement or even replace blood in our circulatory systems. The main reason for such a search is to eliminate the technical problems and medical risks of blood transfusions. The ultimate goal of such research is to discover or create fluids that are alternative oxygen-transport systems. To date, however, no acceptable oxygen-carrying blood substitutes have been discovered, although some hemoglobin-based carriers and non-hemoglobin, perfluorocarbon-based carriers are under investigation.[25] There, are however, liquid volume expanders widely available for medical cases where only volume recovery is necessary. Those systems still rely on the oxygen-carrying capacity of hemoglobin.

After the resurrection we may possibly look forward to life without the double-edged sword of oxygen, which is both life-giving and life-limiting. Our immortal "spiritual" blood will apparently transport absorbed nutrients (Jesus demonstrated that resurrected beings can eat) to the cells of our bodies. Within those cells, glycolysis, the citric acid cycle, and the electron transport chain (or some equivalent system) will break down those nutrients to produce ATP (or some equivalent energy storage molecule). Critically, at the end of a series of enzymatic steps, some very efficient electron receptor will be there to accept that electron and keep the energy-producing system flowing smoothly. At present, we have no clue what that electron acceptor might be—if not oxygen.

Here, as often occurs in that gap between science and religion, we may either choose to stand firmly on the rock of proven scientific knowledge, or to take a "leap of faith" and discover a previously invisible bridge leading across the chasm to the cave of the Holy Grail. What marvelous wonders may await the inquisitive mind that ventures into that cave? Who knows, perhaps by thinking outside the box concerning terminal electron receptors, some young person reading these very words may be *the* person who discovers the ultimate oxygen substitute—the Holy Grail of blood chemistry—and wins the almost certainly, already earmarked Nobel Prize in Chemistry and Medicine for such a life-saving, life-prolonging discovery. Religious belief can often provide the needed faith to go beyond conventional knowledge and open whole new vistas of scientific research.

What we *can* learn about God from this one demonstration of Christ's ability to eat is, in my opinion, enormous. Putting the discussion of oxygen aside, the other implications of Christ's eating fish and honeycomb, I believe, lead us to conclude that immortal, resurrected life is based on cellular life. Before cells were discovered in the seventeenth-nineteenth centuries, people could believe that they—as well as resurrected beings—were some sort of single, indivisible entity. Today, we have a difficult time even identifying with this belief for mortal humans. We now know that we are each composed of over thirty trillion cells—one hundred times more cells in a single human body than there are stars in the Milky Way galaxy. But most people have not applied that same information to the condition of a resurrected body. How would one build such a body without employing the individual building blocks of that body? How does one make a body of flesh and bone without muscle cells and bone cells? How does one make resurrected muscles pull on resurrected bones without causing individual muscle cells to contract—a process that depends on ATP? To me, the logical conclusion is that God is cellular. This discovery, or proposal, if you will, in my mind does not detract from God's infinity, or omniscience, or omnipotence—but it does enhance our understanding of "the only true God" that we might have "life eternal."[26]

Actually, many of the complex sugars we eat are broken down by bacterial enzymes in our gut, not by our own enzymes, which accounts for as much as 30% of our total digestion.[27] It turns out that the bacterial cells in our bodies are roughly equal in number to our own cells, and many are critical to our normal healthy digestive functions.[28] So if resurrected bodies can consume food, are our bacteria resurrected with us? Are there bacteria in heaven or is the celestial kingdom sterile? If we are eating food in the celestial kingdom, where does that food come from? If there is food there, then there must be death of something, and that something—be it fauna or flora—must parish in the process of being eaten. Christ demonstrated that He could not only eat honeycomb, but that He could eat *fish* as well. And if we consume food in heaven, there must be elimination of waste . . .

It's only been over the past twenty years or so that we've begun to appreciate the microbiome living inside us and the vital role it plays in our own health, and we still have a long way to go. Yet compared to what people understood only fifty years ago, we have come a long way. As with everything else, the more we learn, the more questions are generated. As a result, our meager understanding of and questions about the resurrection were much simpler fifty or one hundred years ago—without the cells and the bacteria—than they are now. Nonetheless, even though many questions persist and other questions arise, we now know much more about the nature of God—which He has commanded us to learn—than anyone has ever known before.

This knowledge does not and should not detract from our belief in God. We should always remember the warning in 2 Nephi 9:

> O that cunning plan of the evil one! O the vainness, and the frailties, and the foolishness of men! When they are learned they think they are wise, and they hearken not unto the counsel of God, for they set it aside, supposing they know of themselves, wherefore, their wisdom is foolishness and it profiteth them not. And they shall perish.
>
> But to be learned is good if they hearken unto the counsels of God.[29]

Furthermore, no matter how much we learn about God, we can never know everything—and we were never intended to know everything in this life, for "without faith it is impossible to please him: for he that cometh to God must believe that he is, and that he is a rewarder of them that diligently seek him."[30]

---

1. Luke 24:33.
2. John 20:19.
3. Luke 24:34.
4. Luke 24:36–39.
5. Matthew 28:11–15.
6. Luke 24:33.
7. Thomas, Janet, "Who Are Matthew, Mark, Luke, and John?" *New Era*, January 2007, 18-22.
8. Mark 16:12–14.
9. Thomas, "Who Are Matthew, Mark, Luke, and John?"
10. Bormann, Lukas, "Jerusalem as Seen by Ancient Historians and in Luke-Acts," in *Understanding the Spiritual Meaning of Jerusalem in Three Abrahamic Religions,* vol. 6 of *Studies on the Children of Abraham*, edited by Antti Laato (Leiden, Netherlands: Brill, 2019), 115.
11. John 20:19.
12. John 20:24.
13. Luke 24:30–31.
14. Luke 24:41–43.
15. John 5:30.
16. Doctrine and Covenants 27:5.
17. 1 Corinthians 15:50.
18. Galatians 1:16–17.
19. Ephesians 6:12.
20. Barnett, JA, "A history of research on yeasts 5: the fermentation pathway," *Yeast* (2003), 20: 509–43.
21. Seeley, Rod R., Trent D. Stephens, and Philip Tate, *Anatomy and Physiology*, 8th edition (New York: McGraw-Hill College, 2007).
22. Bernard, Claude, *Experimental Medicine* (New Brunswick, NJ: Transaction Publishers, 1999).
23. Revelation 2:7; 22:2.
24. Matthew 6:19–20.
25. Henkel-Honke, T., and M. Oleck, "Artificial oxygen carriers: A current review," *AANA Journal* (2007), 75: 205–11.
26. John 17:3.
27. Argonne National Laboratory, "Exploring the role of gut bacteria in digestion," *phys.org*, 19 Aug. 2010, phys.org/news/2010-08-exploring-role-gut-bacteria-digestion.html.
28. Sender, R., S. Fuchs, and R. Milo, "Revised Estimates for the Number of Human and Bacteria Cells in the Body," *PLoS Biol*, 19 Aug. 2016, 19:14: e1002533.
29. 2 Nephi 9:28–29.
30. Hebrews 11:6.

CHAPTER 11

DID CHRIST'S RESURRECTED BODY LOOK DIFFERENT?

Peter (as recorded by Mark) recounted, "After that [Christ's initial appearances on the morning of the resurrection] he appeared in another form unto two of them, as they walked, and went into the country. And they went and told it unto the residue: neither believed they them. Afterward he appeared unto the eleven as they sat at meat, and upbraided them with their unbelief and hardness of heart, because they believed not them which had seen him after he was risen."[1] No scripture elaborates as to what the other "form" might have been.

Luke recounted apparently the same experience, "And, behold, two of them went that same day to a village called Emmaus, which was from Jerusalem about threescore furlongs. . . .And it came to pass, that, while they communed together and reasoned, Jesus himself drew near, and went with them. But their eyes were holden that they should not know him....And it came to pass, as he sat at meat with them, he took bread, and blessed it, and brake, and gave to them. And their eyes were opened, and they knew him; and he vanished out of their sight."[2] There is no additional explanation in the scriptures as to what was meant by their eyes being "holden."

The two disciples apparently did not initially recognize Christ for who He was but apparently did not consider Him anything other than an ordinary stranger.[3] The resurrected Christ apparently had the same body configuration as when He was mortal—including lips, teeth, and tongue to speak, legs to walk, and hands to break bread. His closest disciples could not distinguish His resurrected body from a mortal body—even though, in several cases, they didn't quite recognize Him as the Jesus they had known. The disciples on the road to Emmaus thought He was a stranger, whereas, Mary thought He was a gardener.[4] Maybe He appeared to be a different age, very likely with white hair rather than the dark hair they knew, or perhaps there was some other characteristic, but there seems no doubt that he looked completely human. His apostles in the closed room thought they had seen a spirit but He invited them to handle Him.[5] Furthermore, formal logic and the scientific method teach us the principal of parsimony, which states that, without sufficient evidence to the contrary, the simplest explanation—i.e. that Christ looked like a normal human—is most likely the correct explanation.

John stated in the book of Revelation, concerning the glorified Christ, "His head and his hairs were white like wool, as white as snow."[6] Joseph Smith stated of Christ's initial appearance to him that His "brightness and glory" defied all description.[7] Joseph said even of Moroni's visit to him, "Not only was his robe exceedingly white, but his whole person was glorious beyond description, and his countenance truly like lightning."[8] Later, in April 1836, when Christ appeared to Joseph Smith and Oliver Cowdery at the dedication of the Kirtland temple, Joseph made it clear that Christ had white hair: "His eyes were as a flame of fire; the hair of his head was white like the pure snow; his countenance shone above the brightness of the sun."[9]

Even before Christ's death and resurrection, Mark recounted, "And after six days Jesus taketh with him Peter, and James, and John, and leadeth them up into an high mountain apart by themselves: and he was transfigured before them. And his raiment became shining, exceeding white as snow; so as no fuller on earth can white them."[10] Luke recounted the same event, "And it came to pass about an eight days after these sayings, he took Peter and John and James, and went up into a mountain to pray. And as he prayed, the fashion of his countenance was altered, and his raiment was white and glistering."[11]

Given the accounts of the disciples on the road to Emmaus and of Mary in the garden, Christ did not seem to have a white and glistering countenance, because He appeared to be an ordinary stranger or gardener. However, He apparently did not look like His pre-resurrection self. Therefore, it is my opinion that the resurrected Christ had the white hair He would later exhibit, as recounted by John in Revelation and by Joseph Smith, but without the glistening countenance of His transfiguration and as He would later appear to Joseph Smith.

---

1. Mark 16:12–14.
2. Luke 24:13, 15–16, 30–31.
3. Luke 24:18.
4. John 20:15.
5. Luke 24:39.
6. Revelation 1:14.
7. Joseph Smith—History 1:17.
8. Joseph Smith—History 1:32.
9. Doctrine and Covenants 110:3.
10. Mark 9:2–3.
11. Luke 9:28–29.

CHAPTER 12

CHRIST ENTERED A CLOSED ROOM

On the afternoon of Christ's resurrection, He walked with two of His disciples to the village of Emmaus, where "as he sat at meat with them, he took bread, and blessed it, and brake, and gave to them. And their eyes were opened, and they knew him; and he vanished out of their sight."[1] "Then the same day at evening, being the first day of the week, when the doors were shut where the disciples were assembled for fear of the Jews, came Jesus and stood in the midst, and saith unto them, Peace be unto you."[2] Both of these accounts suggest that the resurrected Savior could come and go at will, either vanishing from sight or entering a closed room.

I have always been intrigued by Joseph Smith's account of Moroni's visit to him on 21 September 1823:

> While I was thus in the act of calling upon God, I discovered a light appearing in my room, which continued to increase until the room was lighter than at noonday, when immediately a personage appeared at my bedside, standing in the air, for his feet did not touch the floor. . . . After this communication, I saw the light in the room begin to gather immediately around the person of him who had been speaking to me, and it continued to do so until the room was again left dark, except just around him;

> when, instantly I saw, as it were, a conduit open right up into heaven, and he ascended till he entirely disappeared, and the room was left as it had been before this heavenly light had made its appearance.[3]

This remains the most complete and detailed account of the transportation of a resurrected being of which I am aware.

This description is particularly interesting because it does not describe light as we know it in our modern world. When we switch on a light, the whole room becomes light at the same time and when we switch off the light, the whole room becomes dark—the light does not gather around the light source, leaving the rest of the room dark. The light in this case appears to be some sort of light with which we are not familiar.

Teleportation has been the stuff of myth and science fiction for centuries. In the tales of The Arabian Nights, first written around the 8th century and translated into English around 1706–1721, jinn or genies were able to instantly teleport themselves back and forth between China and Morocco.[4] An 1878 article in *The Capricornian*, a newspaper in Rockhampton, Queensland, described "The Latest Wonder:"

> The Indian journals supply particulars of a new invention whose reality is at least doubtful. The teleport (says a Bombay paper) is an apparatus "by which man can be reduced into infinitesimal atoms, transmitted through a wire and reproduced safe and sound at the other end!" The apparatus consists of a powerful battery, a large metal disc, a bell-shaped glass-house, and a large iron funnel connected with the wire. An experiment, or an alleged experiment, is described as follows: A dog was placed on the metal disc, and a "powerful current" was applied to it; after a while the animal disappeared, and was found at the other end of the wire contentedly gnawing a bone, just as it was doing before it was "transported." Afterwards a boy was experimented upon . . . a Goanese boy, Pedro . . . The current was again applied to the under part of the discs, and the same effect was observed as with the dog. The house was instantly filled with a vaporous man

> whose features and parts were quite distinct until they disappeared. . . . the grin remained even after the body had disappeared . . . but they found him also at the end of the wire. It was then attempted to send the boy and the dog along the wire at once, but by an unfortunate accident the "infinitesimal atoms" of the boy and those of the dog got "mixed" in transit and the result was, that they both looked dreadfully unnatural creatures . . .. It [the Bombay paper] says that by means of the teleport a man will be able to travel from India to England by submarine cable in a few minutes . . . The telephone and the phonograph have opened the way for many novel applications of electricity, but they have not prepared us for such an invention as the so-called "teleport."[5]

In 1897, teleportation and communication became free of the wires when Guglielmo Marconi successfully demonstrated Wireless Telegraphy by sending electromagnetic waves through the air in London, on the Salisbury Plain, and across the Bristol Channel. His demonstrations paved the way for radio and other wireless communication—as well as fueling the imagination of science fiction writers concerning wireless teleportation. For his discoveries, Marconi was awarded the 1909 Nobel Prize in Physics.[6]

Sci-fi teleportation reached its zenith with the television series *Star Trek*, which first aired 8 September 1966, just in time to be another "course" my freshman year at BYU. In that series, a starship *Enterprise* crew member could enter the transporter room and stand in one of the transporters, where we *Star Trek* fans could watch them dematerialize right before our eyes, to be beamed down and rematerialized on the surface of some alien planet. T-shirts were spawned with the slogan "Beam me up, Scotty, There's no intelligent life on this planet."

The physics behind teleportation in sci-fi stories was determined by the scientific hypotheses of the time, and has included such discoveries as electricity, radio waves, radioactivity, black holes or worm holes, and quantum entanglement. Can any of those physics hypotheses help explain how Christ entered a closed room on the evening of His resurrection?

One way to approach this issue is to first ask the question: why can we see through glass but not through walls? When light (photons) strikes a wall, one of two things happens to each photon: 1. A given photon may transfer its energy to an electron in one atom of the wall material. With the added energy, the electron automatically moves to a higher energy level, the photon is extinguished, the extra energy is given off as heat, and the electron then returns to its original energy state. 2. Some photons are reflected by the wall. In this case, the photon again gives up its energy to the wall material, but rather than the energy being captured by an electron, another photon is formed of identical energy and is emitted from the wall.

On the other hand, when a photon encounters glass, it passes through unchanged because the photon does not have enough energy to interact with any electron in the glass. Atoms are about 99.99% empty space. If an atom were the size of a football stadium, the nucleus would be about the size of a marble on the fifty-yard line and the electron orbits would be in the bleachers.[7] The space between the nucleus and the electrons is not uniformly filled with energy. Instead, there are energy bands, and between the bands are energy gaps, where there is no energy at all. Some atoms in some materials have larger band gaps than others. Because of its crystal structure, glass has large band gaps. As a result, the electrons in glass molecules require a much greater energy input to jump from one energy band to another. Photons can pass right through those larger band gaps without affecting the energy levels of the electrons. As a result, most photons in the visible light range (wavelength: 400 to 700 nanometers; photon energy: 1 *hv*, electron volts) travel right through glass without being either absorbed or reflected, thus making glass transparent.[8]

Radio waves, on the other hand, can not only pass through glass but can also pass through walls because they have such long wavelengths and such low energy (100 centimeters to 100 kilometers; photon energy: 10^{-6} to 10^{-13} *hv*, electron volts). As a result, radio waves can pass through the band gaps of most regular matter, such as walls and human bodies, without being absorbed or reflected. On the other extreme end of the electromagnetic scale, X-rays, whose wavelengths are down in the size range of atoms (wavelength: 10 nanometers to 1 picometer; energy: 100 to 100,000 *hv*, electron volts), can also pass through most walls (up to nine-inch-thick concrete). They can penetrate the soft tissue of a human body but not bone, where they are absorbed, thus giving an x-ray picture of bone when passed to a photographic plate. Gamma rays, with even shorter wavelengths, down in the size range of a single nucleus (wavelength: 10 picometer to 10 zeptometers; energy: 100,000 to 1 septillion *hv*, electron volts), but their extremely high energy levels, can interact violently with matter, by ejecting an electron away from an atom, colliding with an electron, or smashing into the nucleus to blast off an electron and a positron.[9]

Once we reach the size range where electromagnetic particles are subatomic in size, such as protons, neutrons, and electrons, we are into the realm where particle accelerators use those particles to smash other atoms. Neutrinos, which are the size of an electron but with no electric charge and little or no mass, even though one of the most abundant particles in the universe, have very little interaction with matter, and therefore are very difficult to even detect.[10]

Dark matter and dark energy, which together make up over 95% of the universe, are not detectable by any techniques so far invented. It is known that dark matter exerts a gravitational force and that dark energy exerts energy, but nothing additional is known about either. It is not clear how or even if dark matter and dark energy interact with regular matter. We have no idea how or even if either may be in any way associated with teleportation.

Joseph Smith has stated that, "There is no such thing as immaterial matter. All spirit is matter, but it is more fine or pure, and can only be discerned by purer eyes; We cannot see it; but when our bodies are purified we shall see that it is all matter."[11]

A vision was given to Joseph Smith the Prophet, in the temple at Kirtland, Ohio, January 21, 1836. The occasion was the administration of ordinances in preparation for the dedication of the Kirtland temple. Joseph Smith reflected, "The heavens were opened upon us, and I beheld the celestial kingdom of God, and the glory thereof, whether in the body or out I cannot tell."[12]

Joseph Smith made no such statement about his first encounter with the angel Moroni as described above. What Joseph Smith witnessed that night is, to my knowledge, completely without parallel in human history. Light does not normally behave the way he described in that incident. In 1823, light was provided by candles or whale oil lamps. Coal oil, or kerosene, lamps were twenty years away and practical incandescent lights would not be available for another fifty-six years. Neither candles nor whale oil lamps were capable of making a room "lighter than at noonday," and incandescent lights, which can make a room lighter than noonday, are either on or off. Incandescent lights neither "continued to increase" nor begin to "gather immediately around . . . [a] person." Even more amazing is the means of Moroni's departure; "a conduit open[ed] right up into heaven, and he [Moroni] ascended till he entirely disappeared." The nature of the conduit was not described, but it apparently went right up into heaven, right through the wall and roof of Joseph Smith's home.

Joseph Smith did not state, when he saw that conduit, whether he was "in the body or out" and whether his body was "purified" so that he could see that it was "all matter." His description of the light and the conduit do not match the behavior of any light or transportation of which I am aware. His encounters with heavenly beings are quite remarkable. Nonetheless, for me, the actual existence of the Book of Mormon testifies to the reality, no matter how remarkable, of its origin.

It is entirely possible that Jesus's appearance to His disciples in the closed room had its parallel to Moroni's visit some eighteen hundred years later. Given the right material, there are electromagnetic particles with both very long wavelengths and very short wavelengths that can pass through walls and roofs without interacting with the material from which they are made, but then, if Christ were made of such material, how was it possible that His disciples could handle Him and see?[13] At this point, even with some powerful hints from modern heavenly visits, and even from modern science, we are still a long way from understanding how the transportation of resurrected beings actually happens. Nonetheless, a testimony of the Savior's resurrection dictates a belief in the various accounts of His post-resurrection ministry among His disciples.

At present, quantum teleportation of humans exists only in the realm of science fiction, but the idea of transporting 525 people in a 1,265,000-pound airplane non-stop from Hong Kong to New York at 652 mph (0.85 the speed of sound) was even beyond science fiction and anyone's wildest imagination one hundred years ago. So was the notion of self-driving electric automobiles or plasma-driven rocket engines made of electromagnets. As a friend of mine, who writes and illustrates science fiction, told me a few years ago: science is moving so rapidly now that science fiction writers are struggling to stay ahead of reality. Certainly no one living one hundred years ago could have imagined that I could look up the world's largest passenger plane on the internet from a computer that fits snugly in my pocket.

Moroni's visitation to Joseph Smith suggests that some sort of light-associated conveyance is involved in teleportation of resurrected beings. Joseph recounted a similar transportation process when the Father and Son first appeared to him: "I saw a pillar of light exactly over my head, above the brightness of the sun, which descended gradually until it fell upon me. . . . When the light rested upon me I saw two Personages, whose brightness and glory defy all description, standing above me in the air."[14]

Maybe teleportation will never become a reality for non-resurrected beings, but that's what they said about the sound barrier. The opening lines of the movie *The Right Stuff*, written and directed by Philip Kaufman in 1983 and based on the 1979 book by Tom Wolfe, are:

> There was a demon that lived in the air. They said whoever challenged him would die. Their controls would freeze up. Their planes would buffet wildly.., and they would disintegrate. The demon lived at Mach 1 on the meter, 750 miles an hour, where the air could no longer move out of the way. He lived behind a barrier through which they said no man could ever pass. They called it the sound barrier.[15]

Chuck Yeager is credited with being the first person to break the sound barrier in the X-1 aircraft in level flight on 14 October 1947, flying at an altitude of 45,000 ft (13.7 km).[16]

---

1. Luke 24:30–31.
2. John 20:19.
3. Joseph Smith—History 1:30, 43.
4. Burton, Richard, *The Arabian Nights*; Canterbury Classics, reprint edition, San Diego, CA 2011.
5. "The Latest Wonder," *The Capricornian* (Rockhampton, Queensland, 29 Jun. 1878), trove.nla.gov.au/newspaper/article/65763678; retrieved 5 Jul. 2020.
6. "Guglielmo Marconi—Biographical," *The Nobel Prize*, nobelprize.org/prizes/physics/1909/marconi/biographical, retrieved 5 Jul. 2020.
7. McCorkle, Kent, "Chemistry Lesson: Structure Of The Atom— Protons, Neutrons & Electrons," *Get Chemistry Help.com*, getchemistryhelp.com/chemistry-lesson-structure-of-the-atom, retrieved 5 Jul. 2020.
8. Harris, William, "What Makes Glass Transparent?" *HowStuffWorks*, 19 Jun. 2000, science.howstuffworks.com/question404.htm, retrieved 5 Jul. 2020.
9. "Gamma Rays in Matter," *radioactivity.eu.com*, radioactivity.eu.com/site/pages/Gamma_Matter.htm; retrieved 6 Jul. 2020.
10. "What is a neutrino?" *Scientific American*, 7 Sept. 1999, scientificamerican.com/article/what-is-a-neutrino; retrieved 6 July 2020.
11. Doctrine and Covenants 131:7–8.
12. Doctrine and Covenants 137:1.
13. Luke 24:39.
14. Joseph Smith—History 1:16–17.
15. Kaufman, Philip, dir. *The Right Stuff*, produced by The Ladd Company (Warner Bros., 1983), film.
16. "Chuck Yeager breaks the sound barrier," *HISTORY: This Day in History*, 27 Nov. 2009, history.com/this-day-in-history/yeager-breaks-sound-barrier; retrieved 5 Sept. 2021.

CHAPTER 13

FLESH AND BONE

The apostle Paul said to the Corinthians, "Now this I say, brethren, that flesh and blood cannot inherit the kingdom of God; neither doth corruption inherit incorruption."[1] We are told in the Doctrine and Covenants that "the Father has a body of flesh and bones as tangible as man's; the Son also; but the Holy Ghost has not a body of flesh and bones, but is a personage of Spirit. Were it not so, the Holy Ghost could not dwell in us."[2] We are further instructed, "There are two kinds of beings in heaven, namely: Angels, who are resurrected personages, having bodies of flesh and bones—For instance, Jesus said: *Handle me and see, for a spirit hath not flesh and bones, as ye see me have.* Secondly: the spirits of just men made perfect, they who are not resurrected, but inherit the same glory."[3] These scriptures have been taken by several leaders of the Church to mean that our bodies of flesh and blood, which are earthly, will be replaced in the resurrection by bodies of flesh and bone, which are immortal.

The Prophet Joseph Smith had this to say about the issue: "As concerning the resurrection I will mer[e]ly say that all men will come from the grave as they lay [lie] down, whether old or young their will not be added unto the[i]r stature one cubit neither taken from it, All being raised by the power of God having the Spirit of God in their bodies & not Blood."[4] President Smith also stated, "God Almighty himself dwells in Eternal fire, flesh and blood cannot go there <for> all corruption is devoured by the fire— our God is a consuming fire— when our flesh is quickened by the Spirit, there will be no blood <in the tabernacle,>— "[5]

In the First Presidency Message of the September 1978 *Ensign* entitled, "Absolute Truth," President Spencer W. Kimball stated,

> A few more salient facts, which I shall not attempt at this moment to elaborate upon: Adam and Eve transgressed a law and were responsible for a change that came to all their posterity, that of mortality. Could it have been the different food which made the change? Somehow blood, the life-giving element in our bodies, replaced the finer substance which coursed through their bodies before. They and we became mortal, subject to illness, pains, and even the physical dissolution called death. But the spirit, which is supreme in the dual man, transcends the body. It does not decompose but proceeds to the spirit world for further experience, with the assurance that after sufficient preparation there, a reunion will take place where the spirit will be housed eternally in a remodeled body of flesh and bones. This time the union will never be dissolved, since there will be no blood to disintegrate and cause trouble. A finer substance will give life to the body and will render it immortal.[6]

Ten years later, in a general conference talk in October 1988, entitled "Funerals—A Time for Reverence," Elder Boyd K. Packer, of the Quorum of the Twelve Apostles, stated: "The word *fall* well describes what transpired when Adam and Eve were driven from the garden. A transformation took place in their bodies. The bodies of flesh and bone became temporal bodies. *Temporal* means temporary. The scriptures say, 'the life of all flesh is the blood thereof.'"[7] He then quoted from the above *Ensign* statement of President Kimball and continued, "After the transformation of the Fall, bodies of flesh and bone and *blood* (unlike our spirit bodies) could not endure. Somehow the ingredient of blood carried with it a limit to life. It was as though a clock were set and a time given. Thereafter, all living things moved inexorably toward mortal death."[8]

Then, in October 1996, in a general conference address entitled, "The Atonement," Elder Russell M. Nelson, of the Quorum of the Twelve Apostles, said,

> The Creation culminated with Adam and Eve in the Garden of Eden. They were created in the image of God, with bodies of flesh and bone. Created in the image of God and not yet mortal, they could not grow old and die. . . . The Fall of Adam (and Eve) constituted the *mortal creation* and brought about the required changes in their bodies, including the circulation of blood and other modifications as well....The Atonement of Jesus Christ became the *immortal creation.* He volunteered to answer the ends of a law previously transgressed. And by the shedding of His blood, His and our physical bodies could become perfected. They could again function without blood, just as Adam's and Eve's did in their *paradisiacal* form. Paul taught that "flesh and blood cannot inherit the kingdom of God; . . . this mortal must put on immortality."[9]

Therefore, from the first prophet of the modern dispensation, the Prophet Joseph Smith, who said, "All being raised by the power of God having the Spirit of God in their bodies & not Blood;"[10] to the most recent prophet of this dispensation, the Prophet Russell M. Nelson, who said because of, "the Atonement of Jesus Christ . . .His and our physical bodies could become perfected. They could again function without blood," we are taught that resurrected bodies have no blood. And this we will continue to believe until such time that there is additional revelation on this matter.

It may simply be that no one has asked the right question. Clayton M. Christensen, in his book, *The Power of Everyday Missionaries*, stated,

> One metaphor that helps me is to imagine that God has constructed massive libraries in heaven. The shelves in these libraries are filled with books that are packed with truths, insights, and answers. Most of the books have never been checked out. Why, you might ask, are these stored in

> these libraries rather than having been distributed broadly to people on earth?
>
> The reason is that people learn when they're ready to learn, not when we're ready to teach them. . . . The rule is this: Anybody on earth can check out any book—but the catch is that you need to ask the question first. . . .
>
> In the third century after Christ's death, the leaders of the early Christian Church essentially announced that God had given them all the answers. And believing that they had received all the answers, there was no need to ask questions of God. When they stopped asking questions, revelation from heaven stopped.[11]

During the 2018 April general conference, President Russell M. Nelson stated, "One of the things the Spirit has repeatedly impressed upon my mind since my new calling as President of the Church is how willing the Lord is to reveal His mind and will. The privilege of receiving revelation is one of the greatest gifts of God to His children."[13] I believe that the revelations leading to the Come Follow Me program for the Church were given us to prepare for a time when we would not be able to attend Church in chapels but would be conducting our own family services in our homes. Little did we know how quickly that program would be needed. Many other revelations will be poured out upon the heads of the Latter-day Saints as we ask questions and patiently await the answers. Revelations for the entire Church will be given, in the Lord's time, to the prophet.

We are told by revelation that God and Jesus Christ have bodies of flesh and bones[13] and that we, as resurrected beings, will also have bodies of flesh and bones.[14] The Savior invited His disciples, "Behold my hands and my feet, that it is I myself: handle me, and see; for a spirit hath not flesh and bones, as ye see me have."[15] We, as yet, do not have many of the answers to the questions such scriptures present, but, nonetheless, we may reason together and ponder what we know from science and what we may seek by revelation.

Let us here, then consider the anatomy and physiology of a body composed of flesh and bones walking out of the tomb to Emmaus and then to Jerusalem. Jesus said, "it is I myself." The Garden Tomb was empty, Jesus Christ testified of His own resurrection that, blood or no blood, His body of flesh and bones walked out of that tomb, walked to Emmaus, and appeared to His disciples in a closed room in Jerusalem where His disciples were allowed to handle Him. He may have shed His blood, but the flesh and bones handled by the disciples on that Sunday night were the same flesh and bones that had knelt before His Father, and our Father, in the Garden of Gethsemane three nights earlier.

The Greek word σάρκα (sarka), is translated as flesh in the New Testament.[16] According to Merriam-Webster, "flesh" is defined as "the parts [of the body] composed chiefly of skeletal muscle."[17] The Greek word sarco- is a "combining form denoting muscular substance or a resemblance to flesh."[18] Sarco- is the root of the word sarcomere, which is the "the contractile unit of a myofibril [muscle fiber, a muscle cell]; sarcomeres are repeating units" of skeletal muscle.[19]

Muscle contraction remained a baffling mystery for most of human history. Indeed, the word "muscle" is late Middle English, which is derived from the French *le muscle*, which is in turn derived from the Latin word *musculus*, which is diminutive of *mus* or "mouse."[20] The best early scholars could do was to hypothesize that muscle movement resembled little mice moving around under the skin. The Greek physician, philosopher, and greatest medical researcher of antiquity, Claudius Galen, better known as Galen of Pergamon, who lived in Rome and was the personal physician to Lucius Aurelius Commodus, heir and successor to Marcus Aurelius; advocated that fluid, transported through the hollow nerves, caused muscles to contract via hydraulic pressure.[21] During the seventeenth century, both René Descartes and Thomas Willis explained that "animal spirits" flowed through the nerves, to the muscles, where "vital spirits" were ignited to produce muscular movement.[22]

Even though Luigi Galvani demonstrated in 1780 that the legs of a dead frog will twitch when stimulated by an electric charge,[23] a demonstration still conducted in physiology teaching laboratories when I was a student, it wasn't until 1952 that the term excitation-contraction coupling was coined by Alexander Sandow to explain muscle contraction.[24] Two years later, Andrew F. Huxley and Rolf Niedergerke in one paper, and Hugh Huxley and Jean Hanson in another, described the sliding filament model of muscle contraction in the same 22 May 1954 issue of *Nature*.[25]

It turns out that the process of changing a thought, in the brain, into an electrical pulse down a nerve, into a chemical signal, and then into a mechanical movement in a muscle is absolutely brilliant. Might we expect less of an omniscient God? The next few paragraphs, which explain what we now know about muscle contraction, is probably already familiar to younger readers because Anatomy and Physiology (A&P) is a common course in modern high school curricula. Older readers, or others with limited A&P background, may find these paragraphs somewhat daunting. For those people, I suggest searching the internet for images of muscle contraction—to help visualize what I will next describe.

The electrical pulse, which is a change in charge across a neuron (a single nerve cell, the Greek word *neuron* means nerve) cell membrane, called an action potential, begins as a "thought" in the front of the brain—such as "I think I'll walk to Emmaus." The action potential generated in one neuron causes the release of chemicals called neurotransmitters between neurons in the brain, the binding of those neurotransmitters to specific receptors initiates action potentials in the receiving neurons. Upper motor neurons in the part of the brain called the motor cortex have very long cell extensions, called axons, that extend down the spinal cord where they release neurotransmitters onto lower motor neurons, generating action potentials in those neurons. Those neurons in the lower regions of the spinal cord have even longer axons (and numbering in the thousands) that extend through nerves to the more than sixty muscles of the hips, legs, and feet. That's where the most amazing transition occurs.

When stimulated by nerves, skeletal muscle fibers contract (shorten) forcefully and then can be stretched back to their resting length by the pull of other, opposing, muscles or by gravity. Axons from the nerves branch within the muscles so that each muscle fiber is innervated by one branch. Muscles require large amounts of energy. Vascular networks deliver oxygen and nutrients and carry away metabolic waste (such as CO_2) produced by the muscle fibers. Each muscle is composed of muscle cells (fibers), connective tissue, blood (or in resurrected beings, some other fluid) vessels, and nerves. Muscle fibers are long, cylindrical, and multinucleated (each cell has several nuclei—the part of the cell containing the DNA). The muscle fibers are smaller in small muscles and larger in large muscles. They vary from 1 mm to 4 cm in length. They have a striated appearance when stained and examined under the microscope, due to light and dark banding.

Muscle fibers each have a cell membrane called a sarcolemma (Greek: *sarco-*, meaning flesh, and *lemma*, meaning husk), which encloses the cytoplasm (cell fluid, also called the sarcoplasm) containing the multiple nuclei and numerous mitochondria (the energy-producing organelles of the cell). There is a huge amount of the oxygen-binding protein myoglobin in the cytoplasm, which gives muscles a red appearance, and transports oxygen through the sarcoplasm. Each muscle has hundreds to thousands of protein strands called myofilaments (Greek *myo-*, meaning muscle), of which there are two types: actin filaments and myosin filaments. When the myofilaments slide past each other, the muscle shortens with force. Myofilaments are bundled together into cables called myofibrils. Each myofibril has repeating functional units called sarcomeres, each about 2 μm long. There are up to 10,000 sarcomeres, connected end to end, in each myofibril.

Actin myofilaments look like two strands of beads twisted together in a double helix. Each bead (called globular or G actin) has a myosin-binding site where it can attach to a myosin head during contraction. There are two long protein fibers attached along the length of each actin myofilament, called tropomyosin, and shorter protein complexes called troponin attached to both the actin myofilament and the tropomyosin fibers.

Myosin myofilaments look like bundles of microscopic golf clubs with every two handles twisted together, and with a hinge region at the base of each head, where the heads can bend relative to the handles. The hinge region bends and straightens during muscle contraction. A single myosin myofilament contains around 300 myosin molecules, half with the heads to the right and half with the heads to the left. The myosin heads have specific regions that can bind to myosin-binding sites on the actin myofilament. Each head also has a specific region which binds adenosine triphosphate (ATP), like a key inside a lock, and which acts as an enzyme to break down ATP into adenosine diphosphate (ADP), a free phosphate (P), and energy. Part of the energy released from the breakdown is used to bend the hinge region of the myosin molecule during contraction and part is given off as heat.

Tropomyosin is an elongated protein that winds along the groove of the actin double helix chain. Troponin has a region that binds to actin, a region that binds to tropomyosin, and a site that binds to calcium ions. Myosin myofilaments slide past actin myofilaments causing them to overlap to a greater degree and causing each sarcomere to shorten. At rest, myosin myofilaments don't extend the entire length of actin myofilaments. Upon stimulation, myosin heads bind to actin sites and sliding begins. Each myosin head binds and releases several times during contraction, acting like a ratchet to generate tension and propel the myosin myofilaments along the actin myofilaments. This shortens the sarcomeres, which, in turn, shortens the muscle.

At the neuromuscular junction (where the axon reaches the muscle fiber), the axonal ending is enlarged, referred to as the axon terminal, and encases numerous synaptic vesicles (microscopic sacs) that contain the neurotransmitter acetylcholine (Ach). The sarcolemma of the muscle cell contains specific Ach receptors. When an action potential in the axon reaches the axon terminal, the synaptic vesicles open to the outside of the axon terminal and release Ach into the synaptic cleft (the tiny gap between the neuron and muscle fiber). The Ach attaches to the Ach receptors on the muscle fiber sarcolemma, causing calcium ion (Ca^{++}) gates to open in the muscle fiber, and resulting in Ca^{++} release into the sarcoplasm.

In the absence of calcium, troponin is attached to both the actin myofilament and tropomyosin, pushing the latter away from the actin double helix groove and up, over the myosin-binding sites, preventing myosin heads from binding to the actin. When a Ca^{++} attaches to the troponin complex, troponin changes shape, pulling the tropomyosin into the actin groove, and revealing the myosin-binding sites. As a result, the myosin head can attach to the myosin-binding site on the actin.

Under resting conditions, ATP is bound to the myosin myofilament heads and the head is bent toward the shaft. As ATP is broken down to ADP, P, and energy, the hinge point straightens out relative to the shaft. With the myosin head straightened out, it attaches to the myosin-binding site on the actin. The release of the phosphate and energy causes the hinge region to bend back toward the shaft, resulting in the power stroke of muscle contraction. With the head bent, ADP is released, another ATP is bound to the head and the head releases from the actin. As long as the myosin-binding site is exposed on the actin myofilament, the myosin heads will extend back out; re-attach to a new site; break down ATP to ADP, P, and energy; and cause the actin and myosin myofilaments to slide past each other—thus shortening the muscle.[26]

I have gone into this much detail on muscle contraction to make the point that muscles contract as the result of very specific chemical interactions. That contraction process is not some magical incomprehensible event (as it had been for thousands of years previously), but is a well-described, known process. Actin and myosin myofilaments constitute 50–60% of each muscle fiber, and 30–40% of a healthy person's body mass is muscle. Therefore, when Jesus arose from the dead and walked out of the Garden Tomb, somewhere between 15–24% of His total mass was actin and myosin. If His walk to Emmaus was powered by some other means than that described above, roughly one fifth of His total body mass was either left behind in the tomb or was now useless. Every statement in the scriptures confirms that the resurrected Jesus neither left any part of Himself behind in the tomb nor was behaving in any manner other than a normal human being—except that He could apparently appear and disappear at will, and He could enter a closed room. Those issues will be dealt with in another chapter.

Therefore, when the Savior invited His disciples to "Behold my hands and my feet, that it is I myself: handle me, and see; for a spirit hath not flesh and bones, as ye see me have,"[27] He must have had a "normal" mouth with which to speak those words. The process of speaking involves muscles just as outlined above for walking muscles. In order to walk and talk, Jesus had to have had a brain to initiate those thoughts and actions, and nerves to carry the action potentials from His brain to His mouth and legs. Thus, having a "body of flesh and bones" also implies a body with a brain, nerves, and muscles.

Furthermore, as described in a previous chapter, the generation of ATP in the mitochondria requires some energy source, such as glucose, and oxygen (or some alternative electron receptor) to be delivered to the muscle cells. Such delivery requires some fluid and carrier proteins, such a hemoglobin, to transport the glucose and oxygen. That fluid, in mortal humans, is called blood and is propelled by the heart. The muscles of the heart work in a very similar manner to the muscles of speaking and walking. There is no reason to suppose that the resurrected Savior had no heart. Therefore, a resurrected body of flesh and bones apparently also has a body with a heart and blood vessels. If that heart is not pumping blood through the vessels, then there must be some other fluid, which replaces the blood in resurrected beings that can carry glucose and oxygen (or some replacement) to the cells and carry waste products—the breakdown products of metabolism, such as CO_2—away from the cells.

An adult body only contains approximately 1.2 to 1.5 gallons of blood, which accounts for only approximately 10% of the total body weight.[28] We are told in the scriptures that, while in Gethsemane, Jesus's "sweat was as it were great drops of blood falling down to the ground."[29] He must also have lost a lot of blood while He was being scourged.[30] Nonetheless, He had to have enough blood in His system to allow Him to walk to Golgotha. Blood would have poured from the nail wounds in His hands and feet. Blood and water came out of the spear wound in His side.[31] It is likely that He may have lost over a gallon of blood total before being taken down from the cross and laid in the tomb. If He finished bleeding out in the tomb the small amount of blood remaining to be left behind when He emerged from the tomb would have been hardly noticeable. There may have been enough blood left in His system to keep His tissue in a vegetative state until His resurrection but certainly not enough to let Him walk out of the tomb.

---

1. 1 Corinthians 15:50.
2. Doctrine and Covenants 130:22.
3. Doctrine and Covenants 129:1–3.
4. "Discourse, 20 March 1842, as Reported by Wilford Woodruff," *The Joseph Smith Papers*, p. [137], josephsmithpapers.org/paper-summary/discourse-20-march-1842-as-reported-by-wilford-woodruff/4, accessed 31 Oct. 2019; see also Smith, Joseph Fielding, *Teachings of the Prophet Joseph Smith* (Salt Lake City: Deseret Book Co., 1976), 199–200.
5. "Discourse, 12 May 1844, as Reported by Thomas Bullock," *The Joseph Smith Papers*, p. [2], josephsmithpapers.org/paper-summary/discourse-12-may-1844-as-reported

-by-thomas-bullock/2, accessed 31 Oct, 2019; see also Smith, Joseph Fielding, *Teachings of the Prophet Joseph Smith* (Salt Lake City: Deseret Book Co., 1976), 367.

6. Kimball, Spencer W., "First Presidency Message: Absolute Truth," *Ensign*, Sept. 1978, 5.
7. Lev. 17:14; see also Deut. 12:23.
8. Packer, Boyd K., "Funerals—A Time for Reverence," Oct. 1988 general conference.
9. Nelson, Russell M., "The Atonement," Oct. 1996 general conference.
10. "Discourse, 20 March 1842, as Reported by Wilford Woodruff," *The Joseph Smith Papers*, p. [137], josephsmithpapers.org/paper-summary/discourse-20-march-1842-as-reported-by-wilford-woodruff/4, accessed October 31, 2019; see also Smith, Joseph Fielding, *Teachings of the Prophet Joseph Smith* (Salt Lake City: Deseret Book Co., 1976), 199–200.
11. Christensen, Clayton M., *The Power of Everyday Missionaries: The What and How of Sharing the Gospel* (Salt Lake City, Utah: Deseret Book Company, 2013), p 30.
12. Nelson, Russell M., "Revelation for the Church, Revelation for Our Lives," Apr. 2018 general conference.
13. Doctrine and Covenants 130:22.
14. Doctrine and Covenants 129:1–3.
15. Luke 24:39.
16. "Luke 24:39," *Bible Hub,* biblehub.com/luke/24-39.htm.
17. "Flesh," *Merriam-Webster.com Dictionary,* merriam-webster.com/dictionary/flesh.
18. "sarco-," *Medical Dictionary for the Health Professions and Nursing,* medical-dictionary.thefreedictionary.com/sarco-.
19. "sarcomere," *Medical Dictionary for the Health Professions and Nursing* (2012), medical-dictionary.thefreedictionary.com/ sarcomere.
20. "Muscle," *Lexico,* lexico.com/en/definition/muscle.
21. Mattern, Susan P., *The Prince of Medicine: Galen in the Roman Empire* (Oxford University Press, 2013).
22. Zimmer, Carl, *Soul Made Flesh, The Discovery of the Brain – and How it Changed the World* (New York: Free Press, 2004).
23. Whittaker, E.T., *A History of the Theories of Aether and Electricity* (Dublin: Dublin University Press, Hodges, Figgis, & Co, Ltd, 1910).
24. Sandow, Alexander, *Excitation-Contraction Coupling in Muscular Response* (Yale J Biol Med., 1952), 25: 176–201.
25. Huxley, AF, and R. Niedergerke, "Structural Changes in Muscle During Contraction: Interference Microscopy of Living Muscle Fibres," *Nature* (1954), 173: 971–973; see also Huxley, H., and J. Hanson, "Changes in the cross-striations of muscle during contraction and stretch and their structural interpretation," *Nature* (1954), 173: 973–76.
26. Seeley, Rod R., Trent D. Stephens, and Philip Tate, *Anatomy and Physiology*, 8th edition (New York: McGraw-Hill College, 2007).
27. Luke 24:39.
28. "Whole Blook and What It Contains," *American Red Cross: Blood Services,* redcrossblood.org/donate-blood/dlp/whole-blood.html, retrieved 4 Jul. 2020.
29. Luke 22:44.
30. Matthew 27:26.
31. John 19:34.

CHAPTER 14

THICKER OR THINNER THAN BLOOD?

Christ's body probably would have been nearly exsanguinated by late Saturday night or into the wee hours of Sunday morning, with an imperceptible pulse and barely enough blood to maintain His tissues in a vegetative, comatose state—certainly, by any ancient, or even most modern determinations, He was dead. But at that moment, by a means that we are still a long way from comprehending, His veins and arteries were infused with some other fluid, some Spirit blood if you will, of which we have no record or knowledge at present, and Christ was changed from mortal to immortal in the twinkling of an eye.[1]

The Prophet Joseph Smith said, "As concerning the resurrection I will mer[e]ly say that all men will come from the grave . . .All being raised by the power of God having the Spirit of God in their bodies & not Blood."[2] Therefore, as a resurrected body has spirit and not blood in the veins and arteries, then that spirit must in some way replace blood in transporting glucose after Christ's meal of fish and honeycomb, as well as oxygen, to His muscle cells where ATP is produced in the electron transport chain to energize His muscles to step out of the tomb and walk to Emmaus and back to Jerusalem. We may wait with some considerable anticipation to discover the details of that other, spirit, fluid carrier that can replace blood. In the meantime, we can exercise faith that the details will be revealed in God's own time and in His own appointed way. So far, over the past seventy years or so, He already has been pouring down an amazing amount of knowledge upon the heads of the Latter-day Saints[3] concerning how a body of flesh and bones actually works. What an exciting time to be alive!

But why stop there? Why stop with just the flesh and bones, with muscle contraction and mortal metabolism? We have been promised by one prophet that God could not be stopped from pouring out knowledge onto the heads of the Latter-day Saints and we have been promised by our current prophet that that pouring out would accelerate right now;[4] all we have to do is open the door to the heavenly library, start pulling down books from the shelves, and start asking questions.[5]

We already have been given a huge golden key. The Prophet Joseph Smith told us in 1843:

> There is no such thing as immaterial matter. All spirit is matter, but is more fine or pure, and can only be discerned by purer eyes. We cannot see it, but when our bodies are purified, we shall see that it is all matter.[7]

So, if blood is replaced by spirit in the resurrection, and if spirit is matter, then we are not looking for some foggy, ethereal substance that is more Victorian mist than the real stuff of science. Rather, we are merely looking for one form of matter replacing another form of matter. Now that's more like it. That's what modern science is all about.

As I discussed in my previous book, *The Infinite Creation: Unifying Science and Latter-Day Saint Theology*,

> In 1901, at a meeting of the British Science Association in Glasgow, William Thomson (Lord Kelvin) described the rotation of stars within the Milky Way galaxy. He proposed that the velocity of their rotation required a much greater mass to the galaxy than could be accounted for by the stars we can see in the galaxy. Thomson thought those "dark bodies" were "extinct," burnt out stars, as did Henri Poincaré, who in 1906 coined the term "dark matter," or "matière obscure" in the original French, to describe them.[7]

Xavier Calmet and Folkert Kuipers have stated very recently,

> There is overwhelming evidence that most of the matter in our universe is dark and cannot be described by the Standard Model of particle physics. . . . About 75% of the matter content of the universe consists of cold, non-baryonic, dark matter. . . . From a theoretical point of view, very little is known of the nature of dark matter. We know that there is no viable candidate in the Standard Model of particle physics.
>
> If we accept that new physics is required to address the missing matter problem, we are faced with a huge theoretical challenge as we have very little information about the nature of the dark matter particle or particles. We do not know their spins, masses, self-interactions or couplings to the Standard Model particles. Furthermore, gravity is universal, it will thus couple to all forms of matter and it will create portals between the Standard Model and any hidden sector.
>
> The lower bound holds for the Standard Model, but it can be relaxed by assuming multicomponent dark matter.[8]

Recently, astrophysicists, using the Hubble Space Telescope and the European Space Agency's Gaia star map, have estimated that our galaxy, the Milky Way, weighs a total of approximately 2.9835 x 10^{39} metric tons.[9] Now, if the galaxy is 75% dark matter—I prefer the original French term "obscure matter"—then that obscure matter weighs somewhere in the range of 2.5876 x 10^{29} metric tons—no trivial amount. Calmet and Kuipers have pointed out that the actual weight of obscure matter will actually fall into a theoretical range with upper and lower limits because the sub-atomic particles composing obscure matter are almost certainly not the same as those comprising standard matter.[10] Indeed, most astrophysicists seem to think that obscure matter particles will turn out to be much lighter per volume than equivalent standard matter.

In 1803, John Dalton promoted the ancient Greek notion that atoms were indivisible and that compounds were combinations of different types of elements. Nearly one hundred years later in 1897, J.J. Thomson discovered electrons, for which he won the Nobel Prize. By

1904, he proposed the "plum pudding" model of the atom in which electrons were scattered in a cloud of positive charge. In 1911, Ernst Rutherford fired positively charged alpha particles at a thin sheet of gold. He found that most of the particles passed right through the foil, but a few particles were deflected at extreme angles. He proposed that atoms are mostly space with a small positive charge in the center—called the nucleus. He later named the proton in 1920. Rutherford also won the Nobel Prize in 1908. Three years later, Niels Bohr proposed that Thomson's electrons orbited Rutherford's nucleus at fixed quantum energies, and he was awarded the 1922 Nobel Prize. Then, in 1926, Erwin Schrödinger, another Nobel Laurette, proposed that the electrons do not move in discrete paths around the nucleus but rather in waves within probability clouds called orbitals.[11]

In 1964, Murray Gell-Mann, working at CERN, the Conseil Européen pour la Recherche Nucléaire (the European Organization for Nuclear Research) postulated the existence of quarks to explain the sub-atomic particles blasted from protons by particle accelerators at the time. Gell-Mann was awarded the 1969 Nobel Prize. Quark theory explains what physicists observe from particle accelerator experiments, leading to the development of the Standard Model, which explains the entire structure of the observable universe. The Standard Model predicts six types of quarks: up, down, top, bottom, charm, and strange—all six of which have been discovered, and three of which, two up and one down, along with three gluons, form a proton. Quarks are differentiated based on properties such as mass, spin, and charge.[12]

Enrico Fermi was a theoretical and experimental physicist who won the Nobel Prize in 1938 for his work on induced radioactivity by neutron bombardment and for the discovery of transuranium elements (those heavier and higher in the periodic table than uranium). He also fled Italian anti-Semitism for the United States the same year. Paul Dirac was an English physicist who shared the 1933 Nobel Prize in Physics with Erwin Schrödinger "for the discovery of new productive forms of atomic theory."[13] In 1926, Fermi and Dirac independently formulated and published what would become known as the Fermi–Dirac statistics to describe the behavior and positions of electrons and protons within atoms.

At present no one has any idea what dark matter, or obscure matter, is. Discussions and hypotheses so far advanced seem to propose that it is a single entity. Even though whatever it is doesn't fit into the Standard Model, everyone seems to want to perform some experiment to make it twist into something that can be deflected into some part of the Standard Model so that some trace of it can be seen. So far, all such attempts have failed.

It appears to me that the most parsimonious model of obscure matter is that of another Fermi–Diracian system with quark-like and lepton-like structures such that there are obscure atoms consisting of obscure protons, comprised of obscure quark-like particles, as well as obscure electrons and other obscure leptons. Such a system would also include an obscure Bose–Einstein system of bosons. Such a system would range from Weakly interacting massive particles (WIMPs) to Strongly interacting massive particles (SIMPs). The system may also include Weakly interacting minute particles (WImPs) and Strongly interacting minute particles (SImPs). After all, at 2.5876×10^{29} metric tons, there should be enough obscure matter to cover a wide range of possibilities.

Those obscure atoms, made up of obscure protons, neutrons, and electrons, would range from obscure hydrogen to obscure carbon and iron, etc. Those obscure atoms, under conditions that we are a long way at present from understanding and which we at present are a long way from controlling, can form obscure molecules such as obscure hemoglobin, which can transport Standard oxygen and obscure serum, which can transport Standard glucose. Such a proposal is absolutely absurd and preposterous except for two things, there are two pieces of concrete evidence to support it.

First, Jesus Christ was placed into the tomb on Friday night with all of His systems intact. His nervous system, muscular system, skeletal system, digestive system, etc. were all intact. Even His cardiovascular system was intact. The one missing component was nearly 1.5 gallons of blood. He had just enough blood to maintain His tissues in a vegetative state and keep them from decomposing over the next few hours. However, He did not have enough blood to support any normal functions—for all intent and purposes He was dead. Then, early Sunday morning, He stood up and walked out of the tomb on His own power. That act required the breakdown of fat reserves in

His body and the transport of glucose from that fat through serum in *new blood*, which had not been there only moments before, to His muscle tissue. That act of walking also required His drawing breath and hemoglobin in the *new blood* transporting oxygen from the air to His muscle tissue. The one missing element in His lifeless body—blood—had to be supplied in order for Him to walk out of that tomb.

Second, Sunday evening Jesus sat down before His apostles and other disciples and ate fish and honeycomb. That act also required the presence of blood with serum to transport the glucose from the digested food to the various tissues of His body. That infusion of blood, in my opinion, came from the vast reserve of obscure matter, which parallels Standard matter, but only interacts during times and under circumstances of which we at present have absolutely no knowledge. As the Prophet Joseph Smith said, "We cannot see it, but when our bodies are purified, we shall see that it is all matter."[14]

The idea that obscure matter might interact with Standard matter might seem absurd until one recalls the statement made by Calmet and Kuipers only months ago that "gravity is universal, it will thus couple to all forms of matter and it will create portals between the Standard Model and any hidden sector . . . assuming multicomponent dark matter."[15]

It is my opinion that God commanded Jesus to eat those fish and honeycomb so that one of the disciples present would recount the experience to Luke, who wasn't there, but who was the only gospel author to record the event, so that someday, two thousand years later, when we had sufficient knowledge to grasp the significance of that event, even though still dimly, those details would be there for our enlightenment.

1. Doctrine and Covenants 101:31.
2. "Discourse, 20 March 1842, as Reported by Wilford Woodruff," *The Joseph Smith Papers*, p. [137], josephsmithpapers.org/paper-summary/discourse-20-march-1842-as-reported-by-wilford-woodruff/4, accessed 31 Oct. 2019; see also Smith, Joseph Fielding, *Teachings of the Prophet Joseph Smith* (Salt Lake City: Deseret Book Co., 1976), 199–200.
3. Doctrine and Covenants 121:33.
4. Nelson, Russell M., "Revelation for the Church, Revelation for Our Lives," Apr. 2018 general conference.
5. Christensen, Clayton M., *The Power of Everyday Missionaries: The What and How of Sharing the Gospel* (Salt Lake City, Utah: Deseret Book Company, 2013), 30.
6. Doctrine and Covenants 131:7–8.
7. Stephens, Trent Dee, *The Infinite Creation: Unifying Science and Latter-Day Saint Theology* (Springville, Utah: Cedar Fort Publishing, Inc, 2020); see also Bucklin, Stephanie M., "A history of dark matter," *Ars Technica* (2017), arstechnica.com/science/2017/02/a-history-of-dark-matter.
8. Calmet, Xavier, and Folkert Kuipers, "Theoretical bounds on dark matter masse," *Physics Letters B* (2021), 814, 136068.
9. Resnick, Brian, and Javier Zarracina, "Scientists weighed all the mass in the Milky Way galazy. It's mind-boggling," *Vox,* 20 Aug. 2019, https://www.vox.com/science-and-health/2019/4/2/18282606/milky-way-mass-stars-dark-matter.
10. Calmet, *Physics Letters B* (2021).
11. Compound Interest, "The History of the Atom—Theories and Models," 13 Oct. 2016, https://www.compoundchem.com/2016/10/13/atomicmodels.
12. MacDonald, James, "A Brief History of Quarks: Understanding the history and future of quarks," *JSTOR Daily: Natural Science,* 20 Aug. 2015, https://daily.jstor.org/brief-history-quarks.
13. The Nobel Prize in Physics 1933, nobelprize.org/prizes/physics/1933/summary.
14. Doctrine and Covenants 131:8.
15. Calmet, *Physics Letters B* (2021).

CHAPTER 15

NICAEA

I have owned my copy of John Laux's *A Complete History of the Catholic Church to the Present Day* for over fifty years, and even though it was written as a high school textbook of Catholic history, I have always found it to be well researched and quite compelling. Laux's (1878–1939) biography on the Amazon books website states,

> He capsulated the Catholic faith extremely well, thanks to his lively prose and succinct way of accurately explaining the details of theology. Though Father Laux originally wrote his books for high school students, they remain very informative for those in college and even adulthood as well. He wrote in a timeless, direct and to-the-point style that continues to present Catholics with in-depth explanations of their faith today.[1]

In his book, Laux admits that the outcome of the Nicaean Council had no scriptural foundation. Of that council, which opened 20 May 325, under the direction of the pagan Roman Emperor Constantine, and was attended by 318 bishops from all over the known Christian world, Laux stated,

> It was proposed to introduce the word *homo-ousios*, which means "of the same essence or substance." Eusebius of Nicomedia objected that it was a technical term not found

> in Scripture. But his objection was overruled: for if Scripture is interpreted in different ways, the Catholics rightly maintained, the Church must explain Scripture by a term outside it. The word homo-ousios (Latin: consubstantialis) was therefore eagerly taken up as just the word wanted; and from that moment it became the watchword of the Catholics in their struggle against Arianism. Constantine himself advised its insertion in the Creed.[2]

It is interesting and important to note that Constantine was not baptized a Christian until just before his death in 337 by none other than Eusebius of Nicomedia. And what was that Arianism, the great Arian heresy, against which the Catholics struggled? Arius, a priest from Alexandria, wrote that,

> If the Son is a real Son, then a Father must have existed before the Divine Son. Therefore He is a creature; the greatest indeed and the eldest of all creatures and Himself a God, but still created; therefore, like all creatures, of an essence or substance (Greek ousia) which previously had not existed.[3]

Although this concept sounds quite logical and straightforward according to the theology of The Church of Jesus Christ of Latter-day Saints concerning Christ's mortal body (what is co-eternal is the intelligence) it was not in agreement with the tangled reasoning of many early Catholic theologians. To them, this "brand of monotheism 'was hardly to be distinguished from that of the pagan philosophers, and that his [Arius'] Christ was nothing but a Greek demi-god.'"[4] Constantine wrote to Alexander and Arius, shortly after 323,

> . . . bidding them cease disturbing the peace of the Church, at the same time giving them to understand that such questions, the meaning of which could be grasped only by a few, had better not be brought into public discussion. This well-meaning attempt at reconciliation, betraying as it did no very deep understanding of the tremendous importance of the issue, came to nothing.[5]

In other words, Constantine, a non-Christian emperor, was dictating to deeply rooted Christian scholars what not to teach because people couldn't understand it—apparently the same people *could* understand homo-ousios. The scriptures seem so clear-cut to those of us in the Church of Jesus Christ. For example, we read in Acts 7 that just before Stephen was stoned to death, "he, being full of the Holy Ghost, looked up steadfastly into heaven, and saw the glory of God, and Jesus standing on the right hand of God, And said, Behold, I see the heavens opened, and the Son of man standing on the right hand of God."[6]

To us this seems very clear. How could Jesus be standing on His own right hand? According to the Catholic catechism, however,

> Henceforth Christ is *seated at the right hand of the Father*: By "the Father's right hand" we understand the glory and honor of divinity, where he who exists as Son of God before all ages, indeed as God, of one being with the Father, is seated bodily after he became incarnate and his flesh was glorified.[7]

If I understand this double-talk correctly, there is only one person seated in glory in heaven. Therefore, what Stephen saw, according to the Catechism, was a metaphor, not two actual people. To this very day, the majority of Christians claim that Stephen "looked up steadfastly into heaven" and beheld a metaphor. Although with his dying breath, Stephen testified that he saw two beings, most Christians do not believe him. Unfortunately, Stephen died and could not contend against the Constantinian heresy of AD 325.

I have read the Catholic Catechism, at least Article I, which begins, "I believe in God the Father Almighty, Creator of Heaven and Earth,"[8] and I find it fascinating—and for the most part accurate. What is missing is a full understanding of the dual nature of God—and us. We are deeply indebted to the Prophet Joseph Smith for the revelations he received clarifying the nature of God and other resurrected beings. Why God chose to wait until 1820 to fully reveal His true nature is a question I have often pondered; and while I understand somewhat the historic context, I am still a child in my comprehension of religious history. Nonetheless, in 1820 God and Christ *did* reveal themselves to the young Joseph Smith, Jr.:

> When the light rested upon me I saw two Personages, whose brightness and glory defy all description, standing above me in the air. One of them spake unto me, calling me by name and said, pointing to the other—*This is My Beloved Son. Hear Him!*[9]

At Nauvoo, Illinois, on 9 February 1843, Joseph Smith the Prophet made known what he called the three grand keys by which the correct nature of ministering angels and spirits may be distinguished. He stated:

> There are two kinds of beings in heaven, namely: Angels, who are resurrected personages, having bodies of flesh and bones—For instance, Jesus said: *Handle me and see, for a spirit hath not flesh and bones, as ye see me have.* Secondly: the spirits of just men made perfect, they who are not resurrected, but inherit the same glory.[10]

Joseph later gave his testimony of the nature of the Godhead at Ramus, Illinois, on 2 April 1843:

> The Father has a body of flesh and bones as tangible as man's; the Son also; but the Holy Ghost has not a body of flesh and bones, but is a personage of Spirit. Were it not so, the Holy Ghost could not dwell in us.[11]

After pondering the word *homo-ousios,* which was introduced at Nicaea in AD 325, and which means "of the same essence or substance," I have concluded that the term is technically correct. Yes, God and Jesus are *of* the same substance—actually substances. They both have a spirit body shrouded in a resurrected physical body. However—and here is the catch—while *homo-ousios* means *of* the same substance, it doesn't have to mean that they inhabit the *same body.* Here is the great Christian misunderstanding of God—the greatest heresy of all time, if you will—that God and Christ are not just *of* the same substance but that they *are* the same substance. This nonsensical notion, which originated in the anti-Arian mists of the early, fourth-century Christian era, is the core creed (being the essence of the Nicaean Creed) which Jesus Christ, Himself, told Joseph Smith "were an abomination in his sight."[12]

Laux has stated that, "The Trinity and the Incarnation are the fundamental doctrine of Christianity."[13] That is why many Christians claim that members of The Church of Jesus Christ of Latter-day Saints are not Christian. My response to that assertion is "thank you" if being a Christian requires me to believe in a nonsensical Trinity.

Coming to the illogical conclusion that God and Christ have the *same* body is like taking the scripture in Genesis 2:24, which states, "Therefore shall a man leave his father and his mother, and shall cleave unto his wife: and they shall be one flesh," to mean that husband and wife are somehow mysteriously fused together into some sort of weird hermaphroditic chimera.

John Laux, to my understanding, very nicely has filled in some of the main events of the third century leading up to the Council of Nicaea. He stated,

> Many Christian teachers, who had no intention of departing from the faith of the Church, set themselves to inquire in what sense was Christ God? Was He God as the Father was God? Was He of the same substance and nature as the Father, eternal as the Father, and equal to Him in power and glory?
>
> Sabellius, an African, and his followers in the third century denied that there were three distinct Persons in God: the Persons, they said, were only like stage characters assumed on different occasions to represent the Godhead to men. This doctrine was rejected by the whole Church because it was clearly opposed to Scripture and Tradition.[14]

I found this information to be very interesting and quite surprising. Growing up in The Church of Jesus Christ of Latter-day Saints, this was always the perception I had of the Catholic/Christian Trinity. Apparently there is more to it than that. Laux continued,

> In his anxiety to establish the distinction between the Divine Persons, St. Dionysius of Alexandria, in the year 260, asserted that the Son was "made by God," and "did

> not exist till He was made"; in other words, he *subordinated* the Son to the Father, just as Justin Martyr and Origen had done before him.[15]

To me this sounds spot on. This doctrine, less than one hundred years later, would become known as the Arian Heresy and would continue to "plague" the Catholic Church for several centuries. Christ himself, in many cases, emphasized that he was subordinate to the Father. For example, Jesus said, "I can of mine own self do nothing: as I hear, I judge: and my judgment is just; because I seek not mine own will, but the will of the Father which hath sent me."[16]

It certainly sounds to me that Jesus is emphasizing that He is indeed subordinate to His Father. But that's not what the Bishop of Rome thought, as Laux explains,

> As soon as it became known in Rome that Dionysius was holding such views, his namesake Pope Dionysius summoned a synod and issued a memorable document to the bishops of Egypt and Libya. "Had the Son," writes the Pope, "been created, there would have been a time when He was not; but the Son always was."[17]

Herein, then, lies the conundrum. Bishop Dionysius declared that the Son was not actually a "son" at all but was as eternal as God. Although through modern revelation, we know that Christ's spirit substance (intelligence) is eternal, as is ours, His organized spirit and mortal body are not. Dionysius served as Bishop of Rome from his election on 22 July 259 until his death on 26 December 268. Nearly a year had passed between the martyrdom of his predecessor, Sixtus II, along with the violent persecution surrounding Sixtus's death, and the election of Dionysius. To Bishop Dionysius fell the task of reorganizing the Church in Rome, which had fallen into great disorder.[18]

Laux uses the term "Pope" to refer to Dionysius, Bishop of Rome. That is not an entirely inappropriate term but, according to Walter Elwell, the term *pope* is derived from a Greek word, meaning "father." During the early Christian era, that term was applied to all bishops, and was only reserved in the Roman Catholic Church for the Bishop of Rome after the 11th century.[19] Why didn't Bishop Dionysius seek revelation in this most critical decision? More importantly, why didn't God give Dionysius the correct information at this time? We cannot simply dismiss the sincerity of Bishop Dionysius. After all, simply becoming a Christian, let alone a bishop, in the third century AD was tantamount to a death warrant. This one concept, the Sonship of the Savior and/or His co-eternal nature with the Father became the basis of an incorrect paradigm and its resultant false doctrine for nearly 1,800 years.

It appears that Bishop Dionysius was of Greek heritage and the idea that there was only one God was held in sharp contrast to the pantheon of Greek and Roman gods. This issue is brought into sharp focus by Paul's speech on Mars's Hill,

> Then Paul stood in the midst of Mars' hill, and said, Ye men of Athens, I perceive that in all things ye are too superstitious. For as I passed by, and beheld your devotions, I found an altar with this inscription, To the Unknown God. Whom therefore ye ignorantly worship, him declare I unto you.[20]

Furthermore, the Israelite religion, from which Christ had risen, was a strongly monotheistic religion. Therefore the early Jewish converts would have insisted upon Christ either being the one true God or no God at all. After all, it had taken years for God to convince the Jews not to worship the multiple heathen gods of the people surrounding Israel—often times not very successfully. One of the most astonishing statements Jesus ever made, one which infuriated the Jews beyond their ability for rational thought and which they considered the ultimate blasphemy, was in the temple at Jerusalem, "Your father Abraham rejoiced to see my day: and he saw it, and was glad. Then said the Jews unto him, Thou art not yet fifty years old, and hast thou seen Abraham? Jesus said unto them, Verily, verily, I say unto you, Before Abraham was, I am."[21]

This declaration harkened back to Moses's calling as a prophet to the House of Israel,

> And Moses said unto God, Behold, when I come unto the children of Israel, and shall say unto them, The God of

> your fathers hath sent me unto you; and they shall say to me, What is his name? what shall I say unto them? And God said unto Moses, I Am That I Am: and he said, Thus shalt thou say unto the children of Israel, I Am hath sent me unto you.[22]

The dialogue between Jesus and the Jews, occupying the entire eighth chapter of John, makes it very clear that even the Jewish *converts* to Christianity[23] did not have a clue about the true nature of God and Christ. Jesus stated over and over that He had been sent by the Father—and then finally, perhaps in frustration at their thick-headedness and pride as the children of Abraham, He asked—no pled, "Why do ye not understand my speech?"[24] Jesus declared that he was the Jehovah, the *I am* of the Old Testament. Then the Jews began to stone him.[25]

After Christ's ascension, the Jewish Christians doggedly continued their old traditions by insisting that converts from paganism be required to live the Law of Moses and be circumcised. Even after Peter's revelation,[26] there still remained debate over keeping the Law of Moses. Paul's letters make it clear that the early Christians struggled with many concepts. While he was in Miletus (now a ruin in modern Turkey), "he sent to Ephesus, and called the elders of the church," and they came to him.[27] He told them that he was bound for Jerusalem and that they would "see my face no more."[28] Then he warned them,

> Take heed therefore unto yourselves, and to all the flock, over the which the Holy Ghost hath made you overseers, to feed the church of God, which he hath purchased with his own blood. For I know this, that after my departing shall grievous wolves enter in among you, not sparing the flock.[29]

In his letter to the Galatians, Paul stated,

> I marvel that ye are so soon removed from him that called you into the grace of Christ unto another gospel: Which is not another; but there be some that trouble you, and would pervert the gospel of Christ. But though we, or an angel from heaven, preach any other gospel unto you than that which we have preached unto you, let him be accursed.[30]

It is obvious from reading 1 Corinthians 15 that the early church members, at least those in Corinth, did not understand the resurrection. Even though Paul tried to straighten them out, the misconceptions remained. Paul expressed his frustration, "Now if Christ be preached that he rose from the dead, how say some among you that there is no resurrection of the dead?"[31] He told them, in frustration, in the opening of his letter, "Is Christ divided? was Paul crucified for you? or were ye baptized in the name of Paul? I thank God that I baptized none of you, but Crispus and Gaius."[32]

But all of Paul's teaching and writing, along with that of the other apostles, could not keep the "grievous wolves" from entering in among the flock.[33] Their stiffneckedness, their thickheadedness, and their self-imposed blindness and deafness, eventually lead to the Nicaean Creed 250 years later, which Christ declared to be abominable.

It took 1,800 years in the wilderness, and the restoration of all things, including a visit from the resurrected Savior, standing beside His tangible and very real Father, our Father and God, for us to now understand what Paul, and Christ Himself were trying to teach in the meridian of time. As a result of this modern revelation, the virgin birth paradox has moved away from the notion that some Pinocchio-like character was born to a woman who was a virgin in the first century AD sense of the term, to an understanding of Christ's necessary cellular composition and the possibility of His conception following some sort of artificial insemination, toward a paradox of trying to grasp how God, therefore, must have 23 chromosomes and 20,000 genes in light of what we think we know about the randomness of evolution.

There is little wonder that Bishop Dionysius, as pious and well-meaning as he must have been, could not overcome the confusion and fog of AD 260 to see the reality of God and His Son Jesus Christ. There was the testimony of Stephen for all to read, yet none had eyes to see through the mists of thick darkness produced by so many years of Greek and Jewish philosophy, in spite of the brilliant writings of the early apostles. Most of the Church Fathers who followed were more content to follow those philosophies of men than the writings of the apostles. It would require another visit from the Father and the Son nearly 1,500 years later to, once again, set the record straight.

1. "About the Author" on listing for "Church History: A Complete History of the Catholic Church to the Present Day," *Amazon Prime*, https://www.amazon.com.
2. Laux, John, *Church History, A Complete History of the Catholic Church to the Present Day* (New York: Benziger Brothers, Inc. Printers to the Holy Apostolic See, 1930), 110.
3. Ibid., 107.
4. Ibid., 108.
5. Ibid., 107.
6. Acts 7:55–56.
7. *Catechism of the Catholic Church,* Part 1, Section 2, Chapter 2, Article 6, Point 663, www.vatican.va/archive.
8. *Catechism of the Catholic Church,* Part 1, Section 2, Chapter 1, Article 1, www.vatican.va/archive.
9. Joseph Smith—History 1:17.
10. Doctrine and Covenants 129:1–3.
11. Doctrine and Covenants 130:22.
12. Joseph Smith—History 1:19.
13. Laux, *Church History,* 104.
14. Ibid., 105.
15. Ibid, 105; italics in original.
16. John 5:30; see also John 5:19; 8:28.
17. Laux, *Church History,* 105.
18. Kirsch, Johann Peter, "Pope St. Dionysius," in *The Catholic Encyclopedia.* Vol. 5 (New York: Robert Appleton Company, 1909).
19. Elwell, Walter A, *Evangelical Dictionary of Theology* (Grand Rapids, Michigan: Baker Academic, 2001), 888.
20. Acts 17:22–23.
21. John 8:56–58.
22. Exodus 3:13–14.
23. John 8:31.
24. John 8:43.
25. John 8:59.
26. Acts 11:1–18.
27. Acts 20:17–18.
28. Acts 20:22, 25.
29. Acts 20:28–29.
30. Galatians 1:6–8.
31. 1 Corinthians 15:12.
32. 1 Corinthians 1:13–14.
33. Acts 20:29.

CHAPTER 16

HERETICS

According to the Catholic historian John Laux, the Council of Nicaea did not see the end of the "Arian heresy," far from it. The Emperor Constantius II, who ruled Rome from 337 to 361, was an Arian. In 355 he convoked a council at Milan where he condemned Athanasius and the Nicaean Creed and received the Arians back into the Church. Several prominent church leaders, including Pope Liberius and Dionysius of Milan, who refused to comply with the imperial reversal, were exiled.[1] Constantius set up a puppet pope, Felix II, for three years until Liberius returned because of pressure from the Roman citizens on the emperor.

By 360, most of the bishops around the world and even Pope Liberius had been forced under threat to sign a modified form of Arianism, called Semi-Arian formula at the Council of Rimini, which left out all reference to substance.[2] Then, in 361, Constantius died. As Laux stated, "Arianism had reached its zenith; its decline was more rapid than had been its rise."[3] The Catholic reaction was immediate. Pope Liberius, in a public letter, condemned the Council of Rimini. Many bishops immediately retracted their signatures. Laux stated,

> St. Gregory of Nazianus . . .in his sermons, especially in the five so-called *Theological Orations*, he dwelt continually on the Catholic Doctrine of the Blessed Trinity, which he set forth with such marvelous clearness and eloquence

> that he earned for himself the title of *the* Theologian and "Defender of the Godhead of the Word." In the short space of less than two years and in the face of the fiercest opposition from the Arian populace, he restored the ascendancy of Catholicism.[4]

On 28 February 380, the Roman Emperor Theodosius I issued an edict, which completely abolished Arianism:

> We will that all the peoples who are ruled by the authority of our clemency shall hold to the religion which the Divine Apostle Peter delivers to the Romans, and which is recognized by his having preserved it there until the present day, and which it is known that the Pontiff Damasus follows, and Peter, Bishop of Alexandria, a man of apostolic holiness, that is to say, that according to the teaching of the apostles and the doctrine of the Gospel, we should believe in one Godhead of the Father, Son, and Holy Ghost, in co-equal majesty and Holy Trinity. We order those who follow this law to take the name of Catholic Christians; all others, mad and insane, we condemn to the infamy of heresy, and they will be punished in the first place by Divine vengeance, and also by our penalties, wherein we follow the will of Heaven.[5]

That edict of AD 380 brought an end to Arianism and marked forever—at least to the present day—anyone who does not accept the Nicaean creed of the Trinity as being "condemn[ed] to the infamy of heresy." My reply—long live the heretic!

Homoousios was the word used at the Council of Nicea to mean the "same substance." It means that the Son is exactly the same substance as the Father and thus is exactly the same person as the Father. *Homoiousios* was the term used by the Arians and other heretics, like myself, and it means "of *similar* substance." It was used by those of us who believed that Jesus Christ is the "Son of God." Notice that the difference in the spelling between the two words is the letter *i*, or *iota* in Greek. Therefore, the difference between a "true Catholic" and a heretic is just one *iota* of difference.

After the edict, those who possessed Arian writings could be sentenced to death. Within six years of making heresy a capital offence, a man named Priscillian, and four or five of his followers, became the first heretics to be executed under the new law. However, Pope Siricius, who opposed Priscillian's heresy, but "believed capital punishment to be inappropriate at best and usually unequivocally evil," excommunicated his accusers.[6] Of course, as time went on, over the next several hundred years, the title of heretic grew ever wider—everyone calling everyone else a heretic and the blade, axe, or firebrand of execution spreading just as wide, as those in power, whether Catholic or Protestant or non-believer accusing the other fellow of being a heretic or witch and dispatching him or her rapidly to heaven or hell.

Heretical accusations were even retroactive. Origen who was known far and wide as the "intellectual leader of the Christians," was condemned by the Fifth General Council in 553 (300 years after his death), because it was determined that his writings included a number of heretical doctrines, such as the pre-existence of souls and the final salvation of all mankind. Such doctrine certainly could not be tolerated by a non-loving disembodied Trinitarian God. Origen, along with the rest of us heretics, must go!

---

1. Laux, John, *Church History, A Complete History of the Catholic Church to the Present Day* (New York: Benziger Brothers, Inc., Printers to the Holy Apostolic See, 1930), 116.
2. Ibid, 117.
3. Ibid, 118.
4. Ibid, 122.
5. Ibid, 122–23.
6. Bassett, Paul M., "Priscillian." in *Encyclopedia of Early Christianity* (2nd ed.), edited by E. Ferguson (Routledge, 2013), 949–50.
7. Laux, 69.

CHAPTER 17

THE RESTORATION

Joseph Smith recounted in his history,

> Some time in the second year after our removal to Manchester [1818], there was in the place where we lived an unusual excitement on the subject of religion. It commenced with the Methodists, but soon became general among all the sects in that region of country. Indeed, the whole district of country seemed affected by it, and great multitudes united themselves to the different religious parties, which created no small stir and division amongst the people, some crying, "Lo, here!" and others, "Lo, there!" Some were contending for the Methodist faith, some for the Presbyterian, and some for the Baptist.[1]

Methodism was begun primarily by John and Charles Wesley at Christ College, Oxford University in the early eighteenth century as a reform movement within the Church of England. They believed that Anglicanism was off course and they pondered the Bible to find the means to right the church through methodical study of scripture and holy living. On 24 May 1738, John experienced an epiphany, as he felt his "heart strangely warmed." Their fellow students mocked them, calling them the "Holy Club" and the "Methodists," being methodical in their Bible study. Three major tenants of Methodism are that:

1. People are by nature dead in sin; 2. They are justified by faith alone; and 3. Faith produces inward and outward holiness.[2]

In the late 1760s, Methodism spread to America. The first Methodist meeting in New York City, and one of the first in the American colonies, was held in the sail loft of a Manhattan rigging house in 1766, with five people in attendance. On Christmas Eve 1784, Methodist ministers of the United States gathered at the Lovely Lane Chapel in Baltimore, Maryland for 10 days and founded the Methodist Episcopal Church. Francis Asbury was ordained an elder and then elected bishop at this gathering known as the Christmas Conference. Asbury was the primary dynamo who drove the spectacular early growth of the Methodist Church in America. He grew up in a middle-class family in England where he dropped out of school because of religious persecution. During his ministry in America, from his ordination in 1784 until his death on 31 March 1816, Asbury ordained some 4,000 ministers, preached 16,000 sermons and traveled 270,000 miles, mostly on horseback.[3]

Alfred Day said of Asbury, "He was a frontiersman and a pioneer. He could have given Lewis and Clark a map to follow before they embarked on their journey and told them which roads to take and which roads were dead ends," bringing Methodism to the most remote corners of the New World. By the end of the century, Asbury's evangelizing efforts had helped make Methodism the largest Protestant denomination in America.[4]

The name Presbyterian comes from the Presbyterian form of church government, where the church is run by representative assemblies of elders, called presbyteries. The Presbyterian Church traces its roots to the Calvinist movement within the Church of Scotland. Presbyterianism was brought to Ireland by Scottish plantation settlers to Ulster who had been strongly encouraged to emigrate by James VI of Scotland (James I of England and Ireland) during the seventeenth century. My Buchanan ancestors were part of this Scotch-Irish emigration. My great, great grandfather, John Buchanan moved at age 14 from Ramelton, Donegal, Ireland to the Pennsylvania in 1800.

Calvinist beliefs, based on the theology of John Calvin, are, first, that of "Total depravity," that is, Humanity possesses a form of "free will," but it is in bondage to sin, until it is at last "transformed."

Second, there is "Unconditional election," in which some lucky souls are chosen by God and everyone else is just SOL. Third, "Limited Atonement," justification is by faith alone, and works are irrelevant. Fourth, "Irresistible Grace," which, is that regeneration, exclusively by the work of the Holy Ghost, is irresistible, whatever that all means. Fifth, "Perseverance of the saints:" that the eternal elect in Christ will certainly persevere in faith.[5] I'm certainly happy for them. And I'm certainly happy that there isn't a test at the end of this chapter. It seems to me that if I were going to church with my great, great grandfather John Buchanan, I would go back home every Sunday quite depressed.

According to Bruce Gourley, who has served as the executive director of the Baptist History and Heritage Society, Baptists most likely grew from within the English Separatist movement, when in the 17th century Protestant Christians separated from the Church of England. The earliest Baptist church most likely originated in 1609 in Amsterdam. The movement then crossed the Atlantic to the New World with the Pilgrims. In America, a former member of the Church of England, Roger Williams (one of my ancestors), was forcefully separated from officials in the Massachusetts Bay Colony over his belief concerning church functions, and in 1638, he founded the first Baptist church in America in the as yet unorganized future colony of Rhode Island. Also in the same area, John Clarke founded another Baptist church around the same time. Both men later received a charter from King Charles II guaranteeing religious freedom in Rhode Island.[6]

By about 1790 there were some 35 Baptist associations in America with around 560 ministers. Estimates put the number of Baptist churches at around 750 and the number of Baptists at around 60,000. Apparently, the Baptist belief in religious freedom was a significant influence in adding the First Amendment to the US Constitution.[7]

Although beliefs may differ among Baptist subgroups, for the most part, as the name implies, Baptists believe in baptism by immersion after a person has professed Christ as their Savior. Baptists believe that the Bible is the only authority for Christian faith and practice. Many Baptists accept the tenants of Calvinism whereas others follow Arminianism, named after Jacobus Arminius, whose teachings say that God has chosen us to bring salvation to everyone, and people have the ability to choose faith.[8]

My fourth great grandfather, Joseph Earl, was a Baptist Minister in Canada and New York. His grandson, James Calvin Earl, after he joined The Church of Jesus Christ of Latter-day Saints, was a member of the Mormon Battalion, along with two more of my great, great grandfathers, John Buchanan, a Presbyterian before he joined the Church, and Alexander Stephens, who may not have had any church affiliation before he joined the Church.

I am not going to discuss the historicity of Joseph Smith's statement concerning the religious fervor in 1818 to 1820, as that is not the purpose of this book, and that discussion is available elsewhere. I will simply continue with his own narrative.

> For, notwithstanding the great love which the converts to these different faiths expressed at the time of their conversion [to Methodism, Presbyterianism, or Baptistism], and the great zeal manifested by the respective clergy, who were active in getting up and promoting this extraordinary scene of religious feeling, in order to have everybody converted, as they were pleased to call it, let them join what sect they pleased; yet when the converts began to file off, some to one party and some to another, it was seen that the seemingly good feelings of both the priests and the converts were more pretended than real; for a scene of great confusion and bad feeling ensued—priest contending against priest, and convert against convert; so that all their good feelings one for another, if they ever had any, were entirely lost in a strife of words and a contest about opinions.
>
> I was at this time in my fifteenth year. My father's family was proselyted to the Presbyterian faith, and four of them joined that church, namely, my mother, Lucy; my brothers Hyrum and Samuel Harrison; and my sister Sophronia.[9]

Joseph Smith continues his narrative.

> During this time of great excitement my mind was called up to serious reflection and great uneasiness; but though my feelings were deep and often poignant, still I kept myself aloof from all these parties, though I attended their

> several meetings as often as occasion would permit. In process of time my mind became somewhat partial to the Methodist sect, and I felt some desire to be united with them; but so great were the confusion and strife among the different denominations, that it was impossible for a person young as I was, and so unacquainted with men and things, to come to any certain conclusion who was right and who was wrong.
>
> My mind at times was greatly excited, the cry and tumult were so great and incessant. The Presbyterians were most decided against the Baptists and Methodists, and used all the powers of both reason and sophistry to prove their errors, or, at least, to make the people think they were in error. On the other hand, the Baptists and Methodists in their turn were equally zealous in endeavoring to establish their own tenets and disprove all others.[10]

Although I said that I wasn't going to comment on the historicity of his narrative, I cannot help but make one comment here. Joseph said in verse 8 that there was "great excitement" and in verse 9 that his "mind . . .was greatly excited." Although one person, or even some people, may say that they can't find much religious excitement in 1820, when Joseph Smith was fourteen, I have had a personal experience with his kind of excitement of the mind, which has remained with me my entire life—over twice as long as his, which has shown me that even though no one else may be excited, one mind may be profoundly excited by a certain event. When I was only eleven years old, there appeared an article, "Where Evolution Stands Today," by Lincoln Barnett in *Life* magazine, 19 October 1959. I'm sure that no one even remembers the series of articles that Barnett wrote, but I do, to this very day, and that series has profoundly impacted my life. Barnett stated, "Today, discovery upon discovery of missing links in the evolutionary chain . . . continues to confirm Darwin's inspired vision, and evolution is accepted by scientists and by mankind in general the world around." I wrote to Barnett, at my tender age of eleven, telling him that I took exception to his statement, " . . . evolution is accepted by scientists and by mankind in general." I, for one, I said, did not accept evolution. At that time, it was said that the entire hominin fossil record could "fit in a shoe box, with room for the shoes." And there were no DNA data linking us to fossil humans. Barnett replied to my letter and kindly encouraged me to pursue my interest in science, which I have—for over sixty years. I have since reversed my view of human evolution 180^0 because of the now overwhelming data—I am a scientist after all. This human fossil record, which could once fit in a shoe box, now fills rooms and the DNA evidence is overwhelming. You may want to check out my website trentdeestephens.com and read my books on the subject—I am still a very active Latter-day Saint. My point here is that it doesn't matter how general or not the excitement was at Joseph's time, it impacted him, and that's what matters. Now, back to the story at hand.

Joseph said,

> In the midst of this war of words and tumult of opinions, I often said to myself: What is to be done? Who of all these parties are right; or, are they all wrong together? If any one of them be right, which is it, and how shall I know it?
>
> While I was laboring under the extreme difficulties caused by the contests of these parties of religionists, I was one day reading the Epistle of James, first chapter and fifth verse, which reads: *If any of you lack wisdom, let him ask of God, that giveth to all men liberally, and upbraideth not; and it shall be given him.*
>
> Never did any passage of scripture come with more power to the heart of man than this did at this time to mine. It seemed to enter with great force into every feeling of my heart. I reflected on it again and again, knowing that if any person needed wisdom from God, I did; for how to act I did not know, and unless I could get more wisdom than I then had, I would never know; for the teachers of religion of the different sects understood the same passages of scripture so differently as to destroy all confidence in settling the question by an appeal to the Bible.
>
> At length I came to the conclusion that I must either remain in darkness and confusion, or else I must do as

> James directs, that is, ask of God. I at length came to the determination to 'ask of God,' concluding that if he gave wisdom to them that lacked wisdom, and would give liberally, and not upbraid, I might venture.[11]

Notice that Joseph Smith never once even mentioned that he was thinking about the Trinity or the Nicaean Creed. Those issues may have been the farthest issues from his mind. All the churches he mentioned in the earlier verses—the Methodists, the Presbyterians, and the Baptists—were all Trinitarian, main stream Protestant churches; no church at the time wasn't—that wasn't even a question on anyone's radar in 1820.

Joseph continues his narrative:

> So, in accordance with this, my determination to ask of God, I retired to the woods to make the attempt. It was on the morning of a beautiful, clear day, early in the spring [apparently 26 March] of eighteen hundred and twenty. It was the first time in my life that I had made such an attempt, for amidst all my anxieties I had never as yet made the attempt to pray vocally.
>
> After I had retired to the place where I had previously designed to go, having looked around me, and finding myself alone, I kneeled down and began to offer up the desires of my heart to God. I had scarcely done so, when immediately I was seized upon by some power which entirely overcame me, and had such an astonishing influence over me as to bind my tongue so that I could not speak. Thick darkness gathered around me, and it seemed to me for a time as if I were doomed to sudden destruction.
>
> But, exerting all my powers to call upon God to deliver me out of the power of this enemy which had seized upon me, and at the very moment when I was ready to sink into despair and abandon myself to destruction—not to an imaginary ruin, but to the power of some actual being from the unseen world, who had such marvelous power as I had never before felt in any being—just at this moment of great alarm, I saw a pillar of light exactly over my

> head, above the brightness of the sun, which descended gradually until it fell upon me."
>
> It no sooner appeared than I found myself delivered from the enemy which held me bound. When the light rested upon me I saw two Personages, whose brightness and glory defy all description, standing above me in the air. One of them spake unto me, calling me by name and said, pointing to the other—*This is My Beloved Son. Hear Him!*[12]

In that moment of sublime revelation, the heresy of 325 and thereafter was swept away from the restored gospel of Jesus Christ to be replaced by the true and matchless understanding of the actual nature of our God and Father and His Son and our Savior Jesus the Christ.

---

1. Joseph Smith—History 1:5.
2. Lovino, Joe, "Roots of the UM family tree: Digging deeper," The people of The United Methodist Church, 3 Jul. 2018, https://www.umc.org/en/content/the-roots-of-the-united-methodist-family-tree-digging-deeper, retrieved 24 Oct. 2021; "Glossary: Wesley, Johm," The people of The Methodist Church, 27 May 2015, https://www.umc.org/en/content/glossary-wesley-john, retrieved 24 Oct. 2021; See also Stebbins, G. and G. King Methodist Itinerant System (Broadside, New York: John Totten, 1810–11), Rare Books Division, The New York Public Library.
3. Ibid.
4. United Methodist Communications, "Methodism's American Saint: Bishop Francis Asbury," The people of The United Methodist Church, 21 Mar. 2016, Nashville, Tennessee, https://www.umc.org/en/content/methodisms-american-saint-bishop-francis-asbury, video, retrieved 24 Oct. 2021.
5. Kraby, Clayton, "The Five Points of Calvinism—Defining the Doctrines of Grace," Reasonable Theology, https://reasonabletheology.org/five-points-calvinism-defining-doctrines-of-grace, retrieved 24 Oct. 2021.
6. Casanova, Amanda, "10 Things Everyone Should Know about Baptists," Christianity.com, https://www.christianity.com/church/denominations, retrieved 24 Oct. 2021.
7. Ibid.
8. Ibid.
9. Joseph Smith—History 1:6–7.
10. Joseph Smith—History 1:8–9.
11. Joseph Smith—History 1:10–13.
12. Joseph Smith—History 1:14–17.

CHAPTER 18

RESURRECTION AND THE HUMAN GENOME

The 16 February 2001 issue of *Science* announced that the human genome project was 90% complete, referring to the human genome as the "Book of Life." The official announcement was released February 12th to correspond with the 192nd birthday of Charles Darwin (not Abraham Lincoln, who was born the very same day). An approximately four foot by four foot fold-out poster of the human genome was included in the issue. I hung my copy of the poster on one of my office walls, where it remained until my retirement ten years later. Two years after the original announcement, on 25 April 2003, to correlate with the 50th anniversary of Watson and Crick's historic paper in *Nature* describing the structure of DNA, the official statement was released that the human genome project was 100% complete.

During the ten years the Human Genome poster hung on my office wall, I often gazed at it, contemplating whether this "Book of Life" might represent the blueprint for the resurrection. The poster did not just show a generic blueprint for all humans, but, rather, most of it (more than 70%) was the blueprint for a *specific, individual* person—a male from Buffalo, New York (code named RP11).[1]

Now, George Church has since set up the Synthetic Biology Laboratory at Harvard University for assembling large genome segments. Church calls his machine an assembly line for DNA—like a

DNA text printer. With this printer, "Humans can preserve their own DNA with the intention of being cloned and reborn after they die."[2]

If human scientists at Harvard can build a DNA printer, assuming Church's project actually works, it doesn't seem like all that difficult of a job for God to build a much more sophisticated printer for giving His spirit children resurrected bodies. The environmental insults, such as thalidomide or alcohol, that cause birth defects, can be eliminated from the heavenly environment and genetic errors in the DNA sequence can be easily corrected, resulting in a perfect human body.

What I don't understand in this whole scenario is the part played by Jesus Christ. I believe in the resurrection of Jesus Christ, I believe in His atonement, and I believe that His resurrection was necessary for our resurrection—I just don't know *how*. The *why* is given to us several times in the scriptures, "For since by man came death, by man came also the resurrection of the dead. For as in Adam all die, even so in Christ shall all be made alive."[3]

I only dimly understand that scripture, but I don't understand from a mechanistic perspective what happens in the resurrection. Probably I'm not *supposed* to know at present. We are told in Hebrews 11:6, after all, that without faith it is impossible to please God. I'm sure there is a lot more information to come, but we also are admonished to *ponder* the scriptures, and I propose to *search* them for every bit of information they can provide. So, what I'm going to do is walk through the events of the crucifixion and resurrection to see what we can glean from the scriptures that at least I may have missed before. We also can perhaps ponder how Christ's resurrection compares to the resurrection of everyone else.

First, I will summarize Christ's conditions after the resurrection, then I will discuss each in detail: 1. His body was gone from the tomb. 2. His resurrected body was in some other form than His earthly body so that disciples who apparently knew Him well did not immediately recognize Him. 3. He exhibited the marks of the crucifixion and spear wound, and invited many witnesses to examine them as proof that He was the risen Savior. 4. He could enter into a closed room without opening the door, and disappear from sight. 5. He specifically said that He had a body of flesh and bones. 6. He specifically demonstrated that He could eat.

1. His body was gone from the tomb.

We read in the Gospel of Matthew:

> And the angel answered and said unto the women, Fear not ye: for I know that ye seek Jesus, which was crucified. He is not here: for he is risen, as he said. Come, see the place where the Lord lay. And go quickly, and tell his disciples that he is risen from the dead; and, behold, he goeth before you into Galilee; there shall ye see him: lo, I have told you.[4]

In Mark we read:

> And entering into the sepulchre, they saw a young man sitting on the right side, clothed in a long white garment; and they were affrighted. And he saith unto them, Be not affrighted: Ye seek Jesus of Nazareth, which was crucified: he is risen; he is not here: behold the place where they laid him.[5]

Then we read in Luke:

> And they entered in, and found not the body of the Lord Jesus. And it came to pass, as they were much perplexed thereabout, behold, two men stood by them in shining garments: And as they were afraid, and bowed down their faces to the earth, they said unto them, Why seek ye the living among the dead? He is not here, but is risen: remember how he spake unto you when he was yet in Galilee, Saying, The Son of man must be delivered into the hands of sinful men, and be crucified, and the third day rise again.[6]

John's account states:

> The first day of the week cometh Mary Magdalene early, when it was yet dark, unto the sepulchre, and seeth the stone taken away from the sepulchre. Then she runneth, and cometh to Simon Peter, and to the other disciple, whom Jesus loved, and saith unto them, They have taken away the Lord out of the sepulchre, and we know not

> where they have laid him . . . Then cometh Simon Peter following him, and went into the sepulchre, and seeth the linen clothes lie, And the napkin, that was about his head, not lying with the linen clothes, but wrapped together in a place by itself. Then went in also that other disciple, which came first to the sepulchre, and he saw, and believed. For as yet they knew not the scripture, that he must rise again from the dead.[7]

Even though the four Gospels differ from one another in the details of what happened that first Easter Morning, they all agree that the tomb was empty. They also tend to agree that His disciples were perplexed, for most did not understand that He had promised He would rise again from the dead. The first three Gospels also agree that one or two angels announced to the disciples, "He is risen."

2. His resurrected body was in some other form than His earthly body so that disciples who apparently knew Him well did not immediately recognize him.

John's account continued:

> And they [the two angels sitting in the tomb] say unto her, Woman, why weepest thou? She saith unto them, Because they have taken away my Lord, and I know not where they have laid him. And when she had thus said, she turned herself back, and saw Jesus standing, and knew not that it was Jesus. Jesus saith unto her, Woman, why weepest thou? whom seekest thou? She, supposing him to be the gardener, saith unto him, Sir, if thou have borne him hence, tell me where thou hast laid him, and I will take him away. Jesus saith unto her, Mary. She turned herself, and saith unto him, Rabboni; which is to say, Master. Jesus saith unto her, Touch me not; for I am not yet ascended to my Father: but go to my brethren, and say unto them, I ascend unto my Father, and your Father; and to my God, and your God. Mary Magdalene came and

> told the disciples that she had seen the Lord, and that he had spoken these things unto her.[8]

This scripture tells us that apparently Mary, who was very familiar with the mortal Jesus, failed to recognize Him even though she saw Him and heard His voice. Only when she heard His familiar greeting, "Mary," did she recognize Him. All four Gospels have told us that the tomb was empty, so Christ's body must have gone somewhere. But that body was either replaced or considerably transformed—we do not know the details, and probably never will in this life. Even with attempts on the part of many authors to explain circumstances under which individual cases may have occurred, the failure to recognize the Risen Christ occurred several times, involving numerous apostles and other disciples. Both Mark and Luke gave an account of Christ's lengthy encounter with two disciples. Mark only mentions it briefly:

> After that he appeared in another form unto two of them, as they walked, and went into the country. And they went and told it unto the residue: neither believed they them.[9]

Luke's account is considerably more detailed and well known:

> And, behold, two of them went that same day [that first Sunday] to a village called Emmaus, which was from Jerusalem about threescore furlongs [about 7 ½ miles]. And they talked together of all these things which had happened. And it came to pass, that, while they communed together and reasoned, Jesus himself drew near, and went with them. But their eyes were holden that they should not know him . . . And it came to pass, as he sat at meat with them, he took bread, and blessed it, and brake, and gave to them. And their eyes were opened, and they knew him; and he vanished out of their sight.[10]

Here again, as with His initial encounter with Mary Magdalene, two disciples, who were apparently familiar with the mortal Christ, had a lengthy interaction with the resurrected Savior without recognizing Him. Mark says He was "in another form," whatever that means. Luke says, "But their eyes were holden that they should not know him,"[11] whatever *that* means. Even while He "sat at meat with them"[12] they didn't recognize Him. Only after He had given them of the broken bread were their eyes "opened" so that they "knew him."[13] Did He have the marks of the nails in His hands while He was breaking the bread? Even when Christ appeared to His apostles, and others with them, "they were terrified and affrighted, and supposed that they had seen a spirit."[14] Why might that be the case? Perhaps, for some unexplained reason, the resurrected body looks nothing like the physical body (for example, as proposed in the 1998 movie, *What Dreams May Come*).[15] I, personally, don't believe this extreme of a change to be the case.

An alternate explanation is as follows: are people resurrected to a specific age? If so, to what age are they resurrected? It is my opinion that resurrected beings are of a "perfect" age.[16] When I was much younger, I believed that that perfect age was around twenty-five. Now that I am considerably older, and have served in the Idaho Falls and Pocatello Temples for several years with some of the most wonderful people in the Church, I have changed my mind about the "perfect" age. I see the beautiful elderly men and women in the temple, with perfect heads of white hair—looking much like President Uchtdorf—and I realize that this is perfection. I certainly do not have a head of perfect white hair (but I'm promised that in the resurrection I have the hope of regaining my hair[16]). When I went to my fiftieth high school reunion recently, some of my classmates, who hadn't seen me since graduation, hardly recognized me and told me I look more like my father than myself when I graduated from high school.

Jesus was thirty-three years old when He was crucified. One possibility is that He was resurrected to the same age—in which case, His closest associates and disciples should have recognized Him. An alternative possibility is that Christ was resurrected to an older, "perfect" age—with white hair, rather than the dark hair He had at age thirty-three, when He was placed into the tomb. Perhaps it was this "older" Jesus that His disciples didn't recognize. There is a problem with white hair, however: hair does not turn white all at once, unless it's bleached or colored in some other way. Rather, hair normally turns white as it grows from the roots.

3. He exhibited the marks of the crucifixion and spear wound, and invited many witnesses to examine them as proof that He was the risen Savior.

During Christ's encounter with Mary and the two disciples on the road to Emmaus, there is no mention of the wounds in His hands and feet. It seems logical that those two disciples would have noticed them as He sat at meat with them. Nonetheless, the resurrected Savior appeared to His disciples in the closed room, apparently as the two disciples who had encountered Him on the road to Emmaus were giving their account to the amazed apostles and other disciples,

> And as they thus spake, Jesus himself stood in the midst of them, and saith unto them, Peace be unto you. But they were terrified and affrighted, and supposed that they had seen a spirit. And he said unto them, Why are ye troubled? and why do thoughts arise in your hearts? Behold my hands and my feet, that it is I myself: handle me, and see; for a spirit hath not flesh and bones, as ye see me have. And when he had thus spoken, he shewed them his hands and his feet.[17]

John filled in more of the story by stating,

> But Thomas, one of the twelve, called Didymus, was not with them when Jesus came. The other disciples therefore said unto him, We have seen the Lord. But he said unto them, Except I shall see in his hands the print of the nails, and put my finger into the print of the nails, and thrust my hand into his side, I will not believe. And after eight days again his disciples were within, and Thomas with them: then came Jesus, the doors being shut, and stood in the midst, and said, Peace be unto you. Then saith he to Thomas, Reach hither thy finger, and behold my hands; and reach hither thy hand, and thrust it into my side: and be not faithless, but believing. And Thomas answered and said unto him, My Lord and my God. Jesus saith unto him, Thomas, because thou hast seen me, thou hast believed: blessed are they that have not seen, and yet have believed.[18]

It is significant that Jesus told Thomas to "thrust" his hand "into my side," as though the spear wound in His side were still open. He did not say, "Feel the scar left from the spear wound." When Christ appeared to the multitude in the New World, He gave them the same invitation:

> Arise and come forth unto me, that ye may thrust your hands into my side, and also that ye may feel the prints of the nails in my hands and in my feet, that ye may know that I am the God of Israel, and the God of the whole earth, and have been slain for the sins of the world.[19]

As late as April 1829, He mentioned the same wounds as evidence of His resurrection.

> Behold the wounds which pierced my side, and also the prints of the nails in my hands and feet; be faithful, keep my commandments, and ye shall inherit the kingdom of heaven. Amen.[20]

Of these wounds, Tad Callister wrote,

> Joseph Fielding Smith made it clear that the prints of the nails in Christ's hands and feet are but temporary, acting as "a special manifestation" to selected groups. When he appears to the Jews in their hour of distress, they will look upon him and he will say: "These wounds are the wounds with which I was wounded in the house of my friends. I am he who was lifted up. I am Jesus that was crucified." (D&C 45:52; see also Zachariah 12:10). When all are judged it seems the reason for his wounds will cease.[21]

It appears possible that Jesus did not have the marks of the nails in His hands while He was sitting at meat with the two disciples at Emmaus, but may have had those marks when He broke bread for them and certainly had them by the time He showed Himself in the closed room.

4. He could enter into a closed room without opening the door, and disappear from sight.

In giving his account of the Savior's appearance to His apostles and other disciples, John emphasized,

> Then the same day at evening, being the first day of the week, when the doors were shut where the disciples were assembled for fear of the Jews, came Jesus and stood in the midst, and saith unto them, Peace be unto you.[22]

Again, when Thomas was there, eight days later,

> And after eight days again his disciples were within, and Thomas with them: then came Jesus, the doors being shut, and stood in the midst, and said, Peace be unto you.[23]
>
> After sitting at meat with the disciples at Emmaus, Christ vanished from their sight.[24]

It is interesting to note in this matter that atoms, such as the hydrogen atom, are about 99.9999999999996% empty space. Apparently, what keeps us from walking through walls ourselves are the negative electron charges in the atoms, not the solid nucleus. It is likely that other, as yet undiscovered, "higher" laws governed the interactions between Jesus's solid, tangible, resurrected body and the walls of the closed room. Which would have seemed less likely to people 2,000 years ago: passing through walls or flying to the moon?

5. He specifically said that He had a body of flesh and bones.

The resurrected Savior invited His apostles and other disciples:

> Behold my hands and my feet, that it is I myself: handle me, and see; for a spirit hath not flesh and bones, as ye see me have.[25]

Joseph Smith would testify 1,800 years later:

> The Father has a body of flesh and bones as tangible as man's; the Son also.[26]

6. He specifically demonstrated that He could eat.

Returning to Luke's account of the two disciples at Emmaus, we read:

> And it came to pass, as he sat at meat with them, he took bread, and blessed it, and brake, and gave to them. And their eyes were opened, and they knew him; and he vanished out of their sight.[27]

While Christ "sat at meat" with His two disciples in Emmaus, did He eat the "meat" or did He just watch them eat? We are not told for certain, but we can imply that as He "sat at meat" He ate with the disciples. A later encounter, however, leaves no question about Christ's ability to consume food. After Christ appeared to the apostles,

> . . . he said unto them, Have ye here any meat? And they gave him a piece of a broiled fish, and of an honeycomb. And he took it, and did eat before them.[28]

It appears that Christ ate the fish and honeycomb specifically to prove to the apostles that He *could* eat. Was this just a one-time event? Did Christ just perform this "trick" to prove He could? It doesn't seem reasonable that Christ would just swallow food to prove that He could. Where did the food go? Did the food go into some sort of container to be surreptitiously emptied once He was out of the apostles' sight—sort of like putting food into some temporary storage compartment of an automaton, or into some magician's magic box? I don't believe that Christ's eating food was some cheap parlor trick. I believe He consumed food to teach us important, eternal truths about resurrected beings—with huge implications.

To me, Christ's purposeful gastrological demonstration provides critical data to our understanding the resurrection. Those data tell us that the resurrected Savior's digestive tract was intact and functional. The Savior did only what His Father told Him to do.[29] Therefore, it appears to me that it is significant to God to let us know that the risen Christ could eat food.

With the data from Christ's appearances after His death in mind, let us next turn to the question of resurrection in general, and ask what Christ's resurrected body can tell us about our future resurrection.

1. His body was gone from the tomb.

The Prophet Ezekiel describes a very strange encounter with dead bodies:

> The hand of the Lord was upon me, and carried me out in the spirit of the Lord, and set me down in the midst of the valley which was full of bones, And caused me to pass by them round about: and, behold, there were very many in the open valley; and, lo, they were very dry. And he said unto me, Son of man, can these bones live? And I answered, O Lord God, thou knowest. Again he said unto me, Prophesy upon these bones, and say unto them, O ye dry bones, hear the word of the Lord. Thus saith the Lord God unto these bones; Behold, I will cause breath to enter into you, and ye shall live: And I will lay sinews upon you, and will bring up flesh upon you, and cover you with skin, and put breath in you, and ye shall live; and ye shall know that I am the Lord. So I prophesied as I was commanded: and as I prophesied, there was a noise, and behold a shaking, and the bones came together, bone to his bone. And when I beheld, lo, the sinews and the flesh came up upon them, and the skin covered them above: but there was no breath in them. Then said he unto me, Prophesy unto the wind, prophesy, son of man, and say to the wind, Thus saith the Lord God; Come from the four winds, O breath, and breathe upon these slain, that they may live. So I prophesied as he commanded me, and the breath came into them, and they lived, and stood up upon their feet, an exceeding great army.
>
> Then he said unto me, Son of man, these bones are the whole house of Israel: behold, they say, Our bones are dried, and our hope is lost: we are cut off for our parts. Therefore prophesy and say unto them, Thus saith the Lord God; Behold, O my people, I will open your graves, and cause you to come up out of your graves, and bring you into the land of Israel. And ye shall know that I am the Lord, when I have opened your graves, O my people,

> and brought you up out of your graves, And shall put my spirit in you, and ye shall live, and I shall place you in your own land: then shall ye know that I the Lord have spoken it, and performed it, saith the Lord.[30]

It is my opinion that Ezekiel's vision of the bones coming together and becoming covered with sinews, flesh, and skin, was an allegorical prophesy of the resurrection after that of Christ. Obviously these dry, disarticulated bones were very different from the body of Christ missing from the tomb. Matthew addresses two events associated with the crucifixion and resurrection:

> Jesus, when he had cried again with a loud voice, yielded up the ghost. And, behold, the veil of the temple was rent in twain from the top to the bottom; and the earth did quake, and the rocks rent; And the graves were opened; and many bodies of the saints which slept arose, And came out of the graves after his resurrection, and went into the holy city, and appeared unto many.[31]

Matthew listed those two events as though occurring close together: the veil of the temple rent and the saints arising from their graves. The latter, however, he qualifies as occurring "after his resurrection" three days hence, and probably, at the earliest, sometime into the following week. It, therefore, appears that the graves being opened and the saints coming "out of the graves," going into the "holy city" and appearing "unto many," is likely a metaphor. Although I believe the last part to be literal—that many people in Jerusalem saw resurrected "saints," I don't believe they literally saw the graves pop open and the saints emerging from them. That would be a very macabre, Victorian, horror movie scene. I believe that the resurrected saints that appeared in Jerusalem after Christ's resurrection were fully perfected, resurrected beings and not some zombie-like creatures from the *Walking Dead*.

2. His resurrected body was in some other form than His earthly body so that disciples who apparently knew Him well did not immediately recognize Him.

The most detailed description of a resurrected being other than Christ was that given by the Prophet Joseph Smith of the Angel Moroni:

> While I was thus in the act of calling upon God, I discovered a light appearing in my room, which continued to increase until the room was lighter than at noonday, when immediately a personage appeared at my bedside, standing in the air, for his feet did not touch the floor. He had on a loose robe of most exquisite whiteness. It was a whiteness beyond anything earthly I had ever seen; nor do I believe that any earthly thing could be made to appear so exceedingly white and brilliant. His hands were naked, and his arms also, a little above the wrist; so, also, were his feet naked, as were his legs, a little above the ankles. His head and neck were also bare. I could discover that he had no other clothing on but this robe, as it was open, so that I could see into his bosom. Not only was his robe exceedingly white, but his whole person was glorious beyond description, and his countenance truly like lightning. The room was exceedingly light, but not so very bright as immediately around his person. When I first looked upon him, I was afraid; but the fear soon left me.[32]

Joseph Smith gave us no inkling of how different Moroni's resurrected body may have been from his mortal body, aside from the fact that he wasn't touching the floor and we have little more information from which to draw conclusions.

3. He exhibited the marks of the crucifixion and spear wound, and invited many witnesses to examine them as proof that He was the risen Savior.

This condition was almost certainly unique to the Savior. Other people will be resurrected in a "perfect" form:

> The soul shall be restored to the body, and the body to the soul; yea, and every limb and joint shall be restored to its body; yea, even a hair of the head shall not be lost; but all things shall be restored to their proper and perfect frame.[33]

4. He could enter into a closed room without opening the door, and disappear from sight.

Again, Joseph Smith's encounter with the Angel Moroni is very informative here:

> While I was thus in the act of calling upon God, I discovered a light appearing in my room, which continued to increase until the room was lighter than at noonday, when immediately a personage appeared at my bedside, standing in the air, for his feet did not touch the floor. . . .
>
> After this communication, I saw the light in the room begin to gather immediately around the person of him who had been speaking to me, and it continued to do so until the room was again left dark, except just around him; when, instantly I saw, as it were, a conduit open right up into heaven, and he ascended till he entirely disappeared, and the room was left as it had been before this heavenly light had made its appearance.[34]

5. He specifically said that He had a body of flesh and bones.

Is there a real difference between flesh and bones and flesh and blood? The resurrected Savior told His apostles and other disciples:

> Behold my hands and my feet, that it is I myself: handle me, and see; for a spirit hath not flesh and bones, as ye see me have.[35]

Paul told the Corinthians:

> Now this I say, brethren, that flesh and blood cannot inherit the kingdom of God; neither doth corruption inherit incorruption.[36]

To ancient Israel, blood had a double meaning. Not only was it the life of the body and it represented the coming Atonement of Jesus Christ, but it also was a corrupting force in the body. The function of blood and how it may relate to resurrection are discussed in chapter 16. In this chapter, I will expand somewhat on the proposed condition after the resurrection. Tad Callister has stated,

> A resurrected body is composed of flesh and bones and spirit, not blood. The prophets have testified that blood, the mortal element that eventually brings death, will one day be replaced by a spiritual substance flowing through our veins.[21]

John Taylor wrote,

> When the resurrection and exaltation of man shall be consummated, although more pure, refined and glorious, yet will he still be in the same image, and have the same likeness, without variation or change in any of his parts or faculties, except the substitution of spirit for blood.[21]

Tad Callister again:

> So spoke the Prophet Joseph: "When our flesh is quickened by the Spirit, there will be no blood in this tabernacle." At that moment "our vile body" shall "be fashioned like unto his [God's] glorious body" (Philippians 3:21). In such a resurrected state one's countenance, one's outer glow and beauty will be but a manifestation of one's inner spirituality—thus, the inner and outer beings will be, in essence, mirrors of each other. Celestial bodies will radiate celestial glory; terrestrial bodies, terrestrial glory; and telestial bodies, telestial glory.[21]

Elder Joseph Fielding Smith, Jr. said in April 1917,

> After the resurrection from the dead our bodies will be spiritual bodies, but they will be bodies that are tangible, bodies that have been purified, but they will nevertheless be bodies of flesh and bones, but they will not be blood

> bodies, they will no longer be quickened by blood but quickened by the spirit which is eternal and they shall become immortal and shall never die . . .blood is the life of the mortal body, but with the body brought forth in the resurrection, which is the immortal body, that is not the case, in it blood does not exist, but the spirit is the life-giving power.[37]

Whereas blood is dealt with in some detail in chapter 14, I'm not sure what more can be added in this chapter. All I can say here is that every prophecy about our resurrection of which I am aware states that resurrected bodies will not have regular blood, but, as President John Taylor has stated, those bodies will have Spirit blood.

6. He specifically demonstrated that He could eat.

The data from the resurrected Christ's gastrological demonstration strongly suggest that resurrected beings have digestive systems where food is pulverized, mixed with digestive enzymes, and where individual nutrient molecules are absorbed through the intestinal cells lining the alimentary canal. In mortals, those nutrients then pass into the intestinal blood supply and are disbursed throughout the body where they are broken down to provide energy for cellular metabolism. It is entirely possible that resurrected beings have some alternative, perhaps parallel metabolic system to ours. Other evidence, however, argues that resurrected beings have cells with chromosomes and DNA, which can interact with ours through the process of reproduction (see, for example, the chapter on the Virgin Birth). The possibility certainly exists that the liquid transport medium, blood, may be replaced by some other liquid in resurrected beings (Spirit blood). At present, we simply have too little information to go any farther.

Actually, many of the complex sugars we eat are broken down by bacterial enzymes in our gut, not by our own enzymes, which accounts for as much as 30% of our total digestion.[38] It turns out that the bacterial cells in parts of our bodies may outnumber our own cells by a factor of ten to one, and many are critical to our normal healthy functions.[39] So are our bacteria resurrected with us? Are there bacteria in heaven or is the celestial kingdom sterile? If we are eating food in the celestial kingdom—where does that food come from? If there is food there, then there must be death of something, and that something—be it fauna or flora—must parish in the process of being eaten. And if we eat there must be elimination of waste.

It's only been over the past twenty years or so that we've begun to appreciate the microbiome living inside us and the vital role it plays in our own health, and we still have a long way to go. Yet compared to what people understood only fifty years ago, we have come a long way. As with everything else, the more we learn, the more questions are generated. As a result, our meager understanding of and questions about the resurrection were much simpler fifty or one hundred years ago—without the bacteria—than they are now.

If the Human Genome Project has given us the human blueprint, "The Book of Life," and George Church at the Synthetic Biology Laboratory can print out copies of us, then what's missing? Maybe what's missing is the link between the bionic body, printed on a 3-D printer at the Synthetic Biology Laboratory, and the spirit which leaves our mortal body at death. At the present time, to my knowledge, we haven't any more clue as to how to reattach our spirit to our body than Peter Pan had of reattaching his shadow. Perhaps that will be the missing link provided by the Savior's infinite atonement. Maybe the Savior's intervention will be the part where quantum entanglement between the body and the spirit is reinstated—we will probably need a lot of help with that part.

---

1. Tuzun, E, et al, "Fine-scale structural variation of the human genome," *Nature Genetics* (2005), 37:727–37.
2. Martin, Thibaut, Anaís Poncet, and J Caitlin Ringness, "Resurrection Science," *XiveTV*, (Gédéon Programmes, 2012).
3. 1 Corinthians 15:21–22.
4. Matthew 28:5–7.
5. Mark 16:5–6.
6. Luke 24:3–7.
7. John20:1–2, 6–9.
8. John 20:13–18.
9. Mark 16:12–13.
10. Luke 24:13–16, 30–31.
11. Luke 24:16.
12. Luke 24:30.
13. Luke 24:30–31.
14. Luke 24:37.

15. *What Dreams May Come*, directed by Vincent Ward (Interscope Communications, 1998) film distributed by PolyGram Filmed Entertainment; film based on Matheson, Richard, *What Dreams May Come* (G. P. Putnam's Sons, 1978).
16. Alma 40:23.
17. Luke 24:36–40.
18. John 20:24–29.
19. 3 Nephi 11:14
20. Doctrine and Covenants 6:37.
21. Callister, Tad R., *The Infinite Atonement* (SLC, Utah: Deseret Book, 2000), 170.
22. John 20:19.
23. John 20:26.
24. Luke 24:31.
25. Luke 24:39.
26. Doctrine and Covenants 130:22.
27. Luke 24:30–31.
28. Luke 24:41–43.
29. John 5:30.
30. Ezekiel 37:1–14.
31. Matthew 27:50–53.
32. Joseph Smith—History 1:30–32.
33. Alma 40:23.
34. Joseph Smith – History 1:30, 43.
35. Luke 24:39.
36. 1 Corinthians 15:50.
37. Smith, Joseph Fielding Jr., In Conference Report, Apr. 1917, 62–63.
38. Argonne National Laboratory, "Exploring the role of gut bacteria in digestion," *phys.org*, 19 Aug. 2010, phys.org/news/2010-08-exploring-role-gut-bacteria-digestion.html.
39. Wenner, Melinda, "Humans Carry More Bacterial Cells than Human Cells," *Scientific American*, Nov. 2007.

ABOUT THE AUTHOR

Trent Dee Stephens, PhD, is an emeritus professor of anatomy and embryology at Idaho State University. He holds BS degrees in microbiology and zoology from Brigham Young University, an MS in zoology from BYU, and a PhD in anatomy from the University of Pennsylvania. He completed postdoctoral training in pediatrics at the University of Washington and has been teaching anatomy and embryology at Idaho State University since 1981.

He was selected as the ISU Distinguished Teacher in 1992 and Outstanding Researcher in 2000. He has published more than one hundred scientific papers and books, and is considered one of the world's leading authorities on the birth defects caused by the drug thalidomide. He has published one textbook (*Atlas of Human Embryology*) and has coauthored fifteen others about anatomy and physiology. He has also coauthored the book *Dark Remedy, the Impact of Thalidomide and its Revival as a Vital Medicine.*

Trent has also authored or coauthored four books on science and religion: *Evolution and Mormonism*, *Who Are the Children of Lehi?*, *The Infinite Creation*, and *The Infinite Fall.*

He has served in numerous Church callings, including bishop twice. He and his wife, Kathleen, serve as temple workers in the Pocatello, Idaho Temple. They have five children and fourteen grandchildren.